COURAGE
TO
STAND

COURAGE TO STAND

Jeremiah's Battle Plan
for Pagan Times

PHILIP GRAHAM RYKEN

CROSSWAY BOOKS • WHEATON, ILLINOIS
A DIVISION OF GOOD NEWS PUBLISHERS

Cover photo: Tony Stone Images

Cover design: Cindy Kiple

First printing 1998

Printed in the United States of America

Library of Congress Cataloging-in-Publication Data

Ryken, Philip Graham, 1966–
    Courage to stand : Jeremiah's battle plan for pagan times /
Philip Graham Ryken.
       p.   cm.
    Includes bibliographical references and index.
    ISBN 1-58134-012-5 (trade paper)
    1. Bible. O.T. Jeremiah—Devotional literature. I. Title.
BS1525.4.R95 1998
224'.206—dc21   98-18646

11	10	09	08	07	06	05	04	03	02	01	00	99	98
15	14	13	12	11	10	9	8	7	6	5	4	3	2	1

CONTENTS

PREFACE

This book is intended to be a practical introduction to the teaching of Jeremiah. I have tried to select some of the prophet's main themes and familiar sayings without losing the thread of his life experience. Small groups and Sunday school classes that wish to use this book will find questions for discussion for each chapter on page 197. Individuals would also find these questions helpful in applying the truths set forth in this book to their lives. For those who want to learn more from this remarkable prophet, a complete exposition of Jeremiah is scheduled for publication in 1999.

Many thanks must be given for the completion of this book. The Reverend Bob Harvey first awakened my interest in Jeremiah. I thank the session, congregation and staff of the Tenth Presbyterian Church in Philadelphia for their prayers, encouragement and assistance. I also thank Dr. Lane Dennis and the staff at Crossway Books for seeing the relevance of a biblical prophet for these pagan times. Most of all, I give thanks to Lisa, Joshua and Kirsten, for the joy they bring to life.

This book is dedicated with gratitude for my grandparents: Albert and Florence Graham, and Frank and Eva Ryken. May God give us grace to live in our times the honorable way they have lived and still live in theirs.

INTRODUCTION

JEREMIAH'S TIMES
AND OUR TIMES

The rabbis called him the "Weeping Prophet." They said he began wailing the moment he was born.

When Michelangelo painted him on the ceiling of the Sistine Chapel, he presented him in a posture of despair. He looks like a man who has wept so long he has no tears left to shed. His face is turned to one side, like a man who has received the blows of many troubles. His shoulders are hunched forward, weighed down by the sins of Judah. His eyes also are cast down, as if he can no longer bear to see God's people suffer. His hand covers his mouth. Perhaps he has nothing left to say.

His name was Jeremiah. He labored as God's prophet for forty years or more, from 627 to some time after 586 B.C. Four decades is a long time to be a weeping prophet.

Jeremiah lived when Israel was tossed among three superpowers: Assyria to the north, Egypt to the south, and Babylon to the east. He served—and suffered—through the administrations of three kings: Josiah the reformer, Jehoiakim the despot, and Zedekiah the puppet. He was prophet during the cold November winds of Judah's life as a nation, right up to the time God's people were deported to Babylon. Jeremiah himself was exiled to Egypt, where he died.

When the indomitable Francis Schaeffer (1912-1984) examined Jeremiah's ministry back in the 1960s, he identified him as a prophet for post-Christian times. "Jeremiah," he wrote, "provides us with an extended study of an era like our own, where men have turned away from God and society has become post-Christian."[1]

The analogy is a good one. Jeremiah's culture was not post-Christian, of course, since Jesus Christ had not yet come into the world. But he lived in a time when people had stopped trusting God. Public life was increasingly dominated by pagan ideas and practices. People still met their religious obligations, but they did so out of duty rather than devotion.

In much the same way, Christianity has lost its cultural influence in the West. With his usual perception, C. S. Lewis (1898-1963) observed, "Whereas all history was for our ancestors divided into two periods, the pre-Christian and the Christian, and two only, for us it falls into three—the pre-Christian, the Christian, and what may reasonably be called the Post-Christian."[2] Recent decades have only served to confirm Lewis's analysis. Many people still go to church, but it hardly matters, to them or to anyone else. There are still Christians, of course, but religion has been excluded from the public square. The twenty-first century thus dawns on a post-Christian America.

How does a Christian live for Christ in a post-Christian culture? The ministry of Jeremiah holds some answers. His courage, his passion, his preaching, even his sufferings show how to live for God when everyone else turns against him. Jeremiah is a prophet for pagan times.

Living for Christ in the twenty-first century begins with recognizing God's personal call to live in these times. Jeremiah did not choose to become a weeping prophet. God chose him: "Before I formed you in the womb I knew you, before you were born I set you apart; I appointed you as a prophet to the nations" (Jer. 1:5). In the same way, the Christian's call to faith and obedience pre-dates his or her existence. God not only knows what he is doing with your life, he always has known. He chose you to love and serve him even before you were conceived.

With God's calling comes God's gifting. Jeremiah was not sure he was up to the challenge of reaching his culture. "Ah, Sovereign LORD," he said, "I do not know how to speak; I am only a child" (1:6). It is tempting to refuse the call when God's work seems too difficult.

This kind of objection, however, has never been persuasive to God. Jeremiah did not get any farther with it than Moses did:

> But the LORD said to me, "Do not say, 'I am only a child.' You must go to everyone I send you to and say whatever I command you. Do not be afraid of them, for I am with you and will rescue you," declares the LORD.
> Then the LORD reached out his hand and touched my mouth and said to me, "Now, I have put my words in your mouth. See, today I appoint you over nations and kingdoms to uproot and tear down, to destroy and overthrow, to build and to plant." (1:7-10)

Not everyone is called to do what Jeremiah did. Every spiritual calling is unique. But the principle holds true: God empowers his servants to do whatever he calls them to do.

God has called and gifted you to serve him at exactly this moment in human history. Jeremiah's example gives strong encouragement to live for Christ in pagan times. At the end of his commissioning, Jeremiah received a promise that applies to every one of God's servants:

> "Get yourself ready! Stand up and say to them whatever I command you. Do not be terrified by them, or I will terrify you before them. Today I have made you a fortified city, an iron pil-

lar and a bronze wall to stand against the whole land—against the kings of Judah, its officials, its priests and the people of the land. They will fight against you but will not overcome you, for I am with you and will rescue you," declares the LORD.

(1:17-19)

CHAPTER 1

GOD FILES

FOR DIVORCE

"If a man divorces his wife and she leaves him
and marries another man,
should he return to her again?
  Would not the land be completely defiled?
But you have lived as a prostitute with many lovers—
  would you now return to me?"
declares the LORD.

JEREMIAH 3:1

I walked past the notice board on the street and I was shocked by my own sermon title, chosen some weeks before: "God Files for Divorce." I ran up to my office and pulled out a Bible to make sure I had it right. God files for *divorce?* Can it be true? Would the God of the eternal covenant end his marriage to his own people?

Yes, he would: "'Therefore I bring charges against you again,' declares the LORD" (2:9). The honeymoon is over. God is taking his people to divorce court. Jeremiah 2 is his legal testimony.

THE HONEYMOON

God remembers what the honeymoon was like. He pages through the photos in his wedding album. As he looks back on the early days of his marriage, there is an ache in his heart. He can remember how his bride adored him when they were first married. "I remember," he testifies, "the devotion of your youth, how as a bride you loved me" (2:2).

God is on the witness stand in the agony of love, the kind of agony Sheldon Vanauken describes in his book *A Severe Mercy*:

> To hold her in my arms against the twilight and be her comrade for ever—this was all I wanted so long as my life should last. . . . And this, I told myself with a kind of wonder, this was what love was: this consecration, this curious uplifting, this sudden inexplicable joy, and this intolerable pain.[1]

Once Israel loved God like a newlywed. Wives should take careful note of Jeremiah's picture of the devoted wife. Actually, the word *devotion* is not strong enough! God remembers the *chesed,* or covenant faithfulness of Israel. This is a word for unbroken promises, unshakable loyalty, unceasing devotion, and unfailing lovingkindness. It is the perfect word to describe marriage because marriage is a covenant relationship. It is more than just a legal contract; it is a steadfast love commitment of fidelity and adoration.

Christians sometimes get the idea that being faithful to God's covenant is simply a matter of obeying God's law. This is because we are legalists at heart. But God never intended our relationship with him to be mere obedience of the will. God wants our hearts as well as our wills. Redemption is a romance.

The children of Israel gave their hearts to God when they first got married. They reveled in the romance of redemption. Like a newly-married bride, Israel loved her divine husband. The proof of her love was following God wherever he led. "Through the desert, through a land not sown" (2:2), this bride submitted to the guidance of her husband. Israel was young and in love, and all she wanted was to be close to her husband. Barren wilderness was not much of a bridal suite, but that didn't matter! Israel followed God out of Egypt, through the wilderness, and into the Promised Land (2:6-7).

If Israel was a loving wife, God was a faithful husband. He did not fail to keep any of his wedding vows. Here husbands ought to take careful note of Jeremiah's picture of the perfect husband.

God had *passion* for his bride. "Israel was holy to the LORD, the firstfruits of his harvest" (2:3a). He took her to love and to cherish. He treated her with honor and respect, setting her apart as holy. Israel was the firstfruits of God's harvest among the nations of the world. She was God's best and most valuable possession, the apple of his eye, dedicated to him alone.

So God *protected* his bride. He would not allow anyone else to taste his fruit. "All who devoured her were held guilty, and disaster overtook them" (2:3b). If anyone threatened Israel or encroached on her territory, God treated it as an attack on his own person. Remember what happened to the Egyptians? Or the Philistines? God saved his wife and kept her safe.

Then God *provided* for his bride: "I brought you into a fertile land to eat its fruit and rich produce" (2:7). God gave Israel a beautiful home. There was plenty of food in the fridge—mostly milk and honey—and fine bone china on the table.

THE GROUNDS FOR DIVORCE

That was then, but this is now. Time to wake up and smell the burnt toast. The honeymoon is over. My wife and I decided our honeymoon was over when the no-stick frying pan we bought when we first got married started to stick. Well, in Jeremiah 2 the frying pan is sticking like the floor of a movie theater.

How could this be happening? If you were there for the nuptials, when Jerusalem was espoused to God, you never would have believed it would all end in divorce. The wedding was so beautiful! The honeymoon was so wonderful! The bride was so devoted! The husband was so faithful! Where did it all go wrong?

God is on the witness stand in divorce court asking the same question: "What fault did your fathers find in me, that they strayed so far from me?" (2:5; cf. 2:31). God did not leave his people, they dumped him. God's people are the ones who have walked out on the marriage. They used to love him, but it's all over now. This is worth remembering whenever God seems distant. As the saying goes, "If God does not seem close, who moved?"

Why would anyone ever move away from God? It makes no sense! Why would a bride leave a perfect husband? Why would she abandon a man who fulfilled all his vows to her? There is no explanation, no excuse. God's bride separated from her husband without the slightest provocation.

God is the one who has been wronged. He is the plaintiff, and this is his accusation: "They followed worthless idols and became worthless themselves" (2:5). This is the only legitimate ground for divorce: adultery (cf. Matt. 5:32). In this case, the adultery is spiritual. God's people have been having affairs with "worthless" idols. This is the same word used in Ecclesiastes for vanity (*hebel*). It means "mist" or "vapor." Idolaters grasp at thin air. Actually, they worship nothing at all.

So the marriage is dying of neglect. God's people no longer seek after God. They no longer say, "Where is the LORD?" (2:6). They no longer recount and recite the mighty acts of salvation. They forget the love that saved them. They suffer from self-induced spiritual amnesia.

This is a reminder for Christians to thank God daily for salvation in Jesus Christ. Recount and recite the saving acts of God in history. Remember what God has done in your life. The road to spiritual adultery begins when you stop reveling in the love of God. Few Christians plan to fall into grievous sin. It is only after falling that they realize they have drifted away from the God of love.

Jeremiah places the blame for Jerusalem's marital difficulties squarely on the shoulders of its spiritual leaders:

> *"The priests did not ask, 'Where is the LORD?'*
> *Those who deal with the law did not know me;*
> *the leaders rebelled against me.*
> *The prophets prophesied by Baal,*
> *following worthless idols."* (2:8)

The prophets, priests, and kings were not part of the solution; they were part of the problem. "As a thief is disgraced when he is caught, so the house of Israel is disgraced—they, their kings and their officials, their priests and their prophets" (2:26). The leaders got caught with their hands in the cookie jar. They were committing secret sins. Like everyone else, they were sleeping around with idols.

The middle of verse 8 ought to keep ministers and other spiritual leaders awake at night: "Those who deal with the law did not know me." A holy calling does not make a holy man. The priests of Jeremiah's day were handling the Scriptures, studying the Bible, and teaching God's Word, but they did not *know* God himself (cf. John 5:39-40). Their ministry was a dead ritual rather than a living relationship.

THE EVIDENCE

Jeremiah 2 does not describe a situation of "irreconcilable differences." This is not a no-fault divorce. God has legitimate grounds for terminating the marriage.

The rest of the chapter gives evidence of the infidelity of God's people. It is like a judicial slide show. As part of his prosecution, God introduces into evidence image after image of spiritual adultery. He lays out his case with the logic of a lawyer and the longing of a lover, proving beyond a shadow of a doubt that his people have forsaken their first love.

What is it like when God's people leave their husband?
Unheard of! Exhibit A: It is like a nation changing its gods.

> *"Cross over to the coasts of Kittim*
> *[Cyprus, in the West] and look,*
> *send to Kedar [a tribe in the far east]*
> *and observe closely;*
> *see if there has ever been anything like this:*
> *Has a nation ever changed its gods?"* (2:10-11a)

Of course not! Travel the world from east to west, no nation
has ever changed its gods. Shoes, maybe, or hairstyles, but not
gods.

Even the pagans are loyal to their gods. They cart them
around wherever they go. Did the Canaanites ever abandon Baal
or Asherah? Never! Did the Babylonians ever forsake Bel or
Merodach? Ridiculous!

> *"Has a nation ever changed its gods?*
> *(Yet they are not gods at all.)*
> *But my people have exchanged their*
> *Glory for worthless idols."* (2:11)

It is hard to believe, but God's people have exchanged the
glorious effulgence of the divine presence for idols made of wood
or stone.

They are so confused they are "cross-worshiping." "They say
to the wood, 'You are my father,' and to stone, 'You gave me
birth'" (2:27). That is, they call the feminine goddess (represented
by the wood) "Father" and tell the masculine god (represented
by the stone) that he gave them birth!

By partner-swapping, Israel has bartered away the living
God. It was a religious crime without precedent in the ancient
world. The pagans never abandoned their dead gods, but God's
people have abandoned the living God. The members of the jury,

namely, "the heavens," ought to be so appalled at what they hear that they "shudder with great horror" (2:12).

What is it like when God's people leave their husband? Exhibit B: It is like leaving a spring of living water.

> *"My people have committed two sins:*
> *They have forsaken me,*
> *   the spring of living water,*
> *and have dug their own cisterns,*
> *   broken cisterns that cannot*
> *   hold water." (2:13)*

Imagine living in the desert. It is always dry. The thing you always need and can never find is water. Then imagine finding a desert spring that continuously bubbles up fresh from the ground. Would you leave a never-ending supply of water behind? Never! Only a lunatic would abandon a desert spring.

Now imagine leaving the spring behind and digging a cistern to catch rainwater. If you went to such trouble, would you leave cracks in the limestone seal? Yet God testifies, "My people . . . have dug their own cisterns, broken cisterns that cannot hold water" (2:13). If leaving a spring is dumb, building a cracked cistern is dumber. It would be like shutting off your water supply and then digging a trench to get water from the nearest industrial canal.

What Jerusalem did made even less sense. God's people were worried about getting squashed by world superpowers. They were afraid of being plundered (2:14-16). So just to be safe, they propositioned their neighbors. They substituted political alliances for their love-covenant with God:

> *"Now why go to Egypt*
> *   to drink water from the Shihor?*
> *And why go to Assyria*
> *   to drink water from the River?" (2:18; cf. v. 36)*

Defense treaties with Egypt and Assyria are like broken cisterns. They cannot hold water the way God can. Worse still, their water turns out to have a bitter aftertaste compared to the sweet living water from God's eternal wellspring. "'Consider then and realize how evil and bitter it is for you when you forsake the LORD your God and have no awe of me,' declares the Lord, the LORD Almighty" (2:19b).

This is partly a lesson about the coming Messiah. No water can compare with the living water God pours out in Jesus Christ (John 4:10).

It is also a lesson about God and country. Politics is a broken cistern. When Christians start to trust in political solutions to save the nation, they bring judgment on themselves. One reason for the precipitous decline of the mainline church in America has been its engagement in liberal politics. By aligning itself with the right-wing agenda, the conservative church has fallen into the same trap. The quest for political power destroys the spiritual influence of the church.

Next comes Exhibit C: When God's people leave their husband it is like a beast breaking free from its yoke.

> *"Long ago you broke off your yoke*
> *and tore off your bonds;*
> *you said, 'I will not serve you!'"* (2:20a)

Jerusalem is like a wild ox that has smashed its yoke against the barn and run off into the fields. On their way into the spiritual wilderness, God's people yell back over their shoulders, "We will not serve you!" Or again, "We are free to roam; we will come to you no more" (2:31).

God's people were made to serve him. To reject servanthood is not freedom, but bondage. Anyone who knows Christ has put his shoulder to the easy yoke (Matt. 11:30). Breaking that yoke to go off and sin is hard slavery.

What is it like when God's people leave their husband? Exhibit D: It is like a prostitute on the street corner waiting for some action.

> *"Indeed, on every high hill*
> *and under every spreading tree*
> *you lay down as a prostitute."* (2:20b)

God's people are guilty of religious prostitution. They have been shacking up with gods they hardly know.

Very likely this refers to Baal worship, which included ritual prostitution at leafy hilltop shrines. The people of Jerusalem had been seduced by the gods and goddesses of Canaan. They were becoming adept at idol worship. "How skilled you are at pursuing love! Even the worst of women can learn from your ways" (2:33). The Jews knew enough about worshiping idols to give lessons to the most experienced pagan.

This was scandalous, as it always is when religious people turn away from the Lord. A regular churchgoer who does not worship God from the heart is more wicked than an unbeliever who has never heard the Gospel. The pagan has no need to teach the apostate about sin.

MORE EVIDENCE

When God's people forsake him, it is also like a wild vine. This is Exhibit E:

> *"I had planted you like a choice vine*
> *of sound and reliable stock.*
> *How then did you turn against me*
> *into a corrupt, wild vine?"* (2:21)

Usually, animals are the ones who turn on their masters; this time it is a plant. Back in the springtime, when God planted his garden, he took some cuttings and planted "a choice vine." He was expecting to get rich, red grapes from the vine and, as one writer describes it, squeeze them into a nice bottle of Sorek wine from the Wadi al-Sarar.[2] But the vine turned on him. God's people are supposed to be fruitful branches of the true vine, Jesus Christ (John 15:1-8). But when they forsook their first love, they went back to their wild natural state and yielded sour fruit.

What is it like when God's people leave their husband? Exhibit F: It is like an indelible stain.

> *"Although you wash yourself with soda*
> *and use an abundance of soap,*
> *the stain of your guilt is still before me,"*
> *declares the Sovereign* LORD. (2:22)

Sin is not simply a cosmetic problem. Even after the detergent, the exotic cleansers, the turpentine and the tomato juice, the stain of sin remains. What soap can wash away sin from the soul? There is no home remedy to take away guilt. Only the blood of Jesus Christ can purify us from all sin (cf. 1 John 1:7).

When God's people leave their husband, it is like a young camel running loose in the desert, which is Exhibit G:

> *"See how you behaved in the valley;*
> *consider what you have done.*
> *You are a swift she-camel*
> *running here and there."* (2:23)

Listen to this description of a young camel:

> Literally, this camel is criss-crossing her tracks. The young camel is the perfect illustration for all that is "skittery" and unreliable. It is ungainly in the extreme and runs off in any direction at the slightest provocation, much to the fury of the camel-driver. To sit in a village courtyard and watch such a young camel go scooting through, with some alarmed peasant dashing madly after it, is an unforgettable

experience; such a young camel never takes more than about three steps in any direction. To this day the young camel provides a dramatic illustration for anything unreliable. Thus "interlacing her paths" is an accurate description of a young camel—it provides Jeremiah a perfect illustration for the fickleness of Israel.[3]

Jeremiah's point is that God's people run all over the place to sin. They are unable to decide which god they want to serve. The reference to the valley is particularly ominous, since it probably refers to the Valley of Ben Hinnom, where children were sacrificed to Molech (2:23; cf. 7:30-32). There is a further reference to murder when God says his people have "the lifeblood of the innocent poor" on their skirts (2:34). The people of Jerusalem practiced both child sacrifice and the systematic abuse of the urban poor. When God is forbidden, everything is permissible, as abortion and the lack of concern about poverty in the pagan West now confirm.

For Exhibit H God moves from dromedaries to donkeys. To forsake him is to behave like a donkey in heat,

> *"a wild donkey accustomed to the desert,*
> *sniffing the wind in her craving—*
> *in her heat who can restrain her?"* (2:24a)

Sin is like the uncontrollable sexual urge of an animal.

> The habits of the female [donkey] in heat are dramatic and vulgar. She sniffs the path in front of her, trying to pick up her scent of a male (from his urine). When she finds it, she rubs her nose in the dust and then straightens her neck, and with head high, closes her nostrils and "sniffs the wind." What she is really doing is *sniffing* the dust which is soaked with the urine of a male [donkey]. With her neck stretched to the utmost, she slowly draws in a long, deep breath, then lets out an earthshaking bray and doubles her pace, racing down the road in search of the male.[4]

Idols do not need to chase the people of Jerusalem. "Any males that pursue her need not tire themselves; at mating time they will find her" (2:24b). God's people were looking for some action. They will find their own way to the temples of the pagan gods.

This shows the power of addictive sin:

> "Do not run until your feet are bare
> and your throat is dry.
> But you said, 'It's no use!
> I love foreign gods,
> and I must go after them.'" (2:25)

Those who are compulsive gamblers, or drug-addicts, or habitual sex-offenders run after their sins until they are barefoot and thirsty. They can hardly help themselves. They crave their addictions and are incapable of giving them up. "It's no use," they say. "I must have my sins."

God's testimony is almost finished, but he has one final piece of evidence, Exhibit I:

> "Does a maiden forget her jewelry,
> a bride her wedding ornaments?
> Yet my people have forgotten me,
> days without number." (2:32)

It would be unthinkable for a bride to forget her wedding dress. Ask any bride what she wore on her wedding day, what her wedding ring was like and how her hair was done, and she will tell you. Yet God's bride has forgotten her husband. All comparisons fail. No wife has ever been this forgetful.

THE DEFENSE

All the evidence has been heard. What is the verdict? Is there enough evidence for a conviction?

Enough evidence!?!? God can make this accusation stick like taffy on a two-year-old! He has every right to sue for divorce.

Jerusalem has no defense. Like most guilty parties, however, she tries to defend herself anyway. Throughout chapter 2, God's bride tries to mount a defense in her own behalf. She protests her innocence: "I am not defiled; I have not run after the Baals" (2:23). But her lie is exposed during cross-examination. She admits that she loves foreign gods (2:25). How fickle! Yet still another claim of innocence follows: "I am innocent; he is not angry with me. . . . I have not sinned" (2:35).

Worse still, Jerusalem is starting to play the blame game, as often happens when marriages start to fall apart. Each spouse refuses to take responsibility for his or her own actions. In this case, Jerusalem has been doing all the cheating, but she has the audacity to bring charges against her husband. "'Why do you bring charges against me? You have all rebelled against me' declares the LORD" (2:29).

In the end, Judah's plea of innocence leads to her condemnation. "I will pass judgment on you because you say, 'I have not sinned'" (2:35). God is not only the spurned husband and the prosecuting attorney, he is also the righteous judge. He weighs all the evidence and renders his verdict: guilty as charged.

The question to ask is this: What verdict would God render about the contemporary church? The dominant sin of Jerusalem—forgetting God—has become a predominant sin in the American church.

Ray Ortlund imagines what the evangelical church would look like without the Gospel:

What might our evangelicalism, without the evangel, look like? We would have to replace the centrality of the gospel with something else, naturally. So what might take the place of the gospel in our sermons and books and cassette tapes and Sunday school classes and home Bible studies, and above all, in our hearts?[5]

Ortlund suggests a number of substitutes for the Gospel. A "drive toward church growth." "Or sympathetic, empathetic, thickly-honeyed cultivation of interpersonal relationships." "Or a determination to take America back to its Christian roots through political power."[6] Or, one might add, any number of otherwise good things that now usurp the throne of a forgotten God.

To make the question personal, What verdict do you deserve? Do you love God like a newlywed, or have you been looking for love in all the wrong places? Whether forgetting God is compared to changing gods, or getting water from a broken cistern, or sleeping around with idols, the sin is the same. So is the verdict: guilty.

THE RECONCILIATION

So God goes through with the divorce, right? He certainly has every right to. The marriage seems beyond recovery.

But it isn't. Just half a chapter later Jeremiah writes, "'Return, faithless people,' declares the LORD, 'for I am your husband'" (3:14). It is a breathtaking command. It is the grace of God to the ungracious, his faithfulness to the unfaithful. Even when God's love goes unrequited he does not cease to love. Although his marriage is violated, he does not break covenant.

If you have never entered into a love relationship with God, he is courting you at this moment. He invites you to enter into a love that will never let you go. He calls you to leave behind the sins that carry you here, there, and everywhere in the spiritual desert. He invites you to embrace Jesus Christ.

If you have already entered the romance of redemption, consider whether you love God the way you did when you first "got married." If not, do not try to dance around this betrayal. If you are not passionately in love with God, then you have been behaving like a floozy, spiritually speaking. But your divine husband still wants you back. More amazing still, he can restore the passion and purity of your love for him.

There is a hint of such restoration later in Jeremiah's book:

> The LORD appeared to us in the past, saying:
> "I have loved you with an everlasting love;
> I have drawn you with loving-kindness.
> I will build you up again and you will be rebuilt,
> O Virgin Israel." (31:3-4; cf. 31:21)

It is amazing enough that God still considers Israel his bride. But there is more. His cleansing is so complete that he restores her to passion and purity.

How can he do that? What detergent can wash away the stain of sin? Nothing but the blood of Jesus: "Christ loved the church and gave himself up for her to make her holy, cleansing her by the washing with water through the word, and to present her to himself as a radiant church, without stain or wrinkle or any other blemish, but holy and blameless" (Eph. 5:25b-27; cf. Rev. 21:2, 9). Jesus Christ died on the cross to remove the promiscuity and restore the virginity of his spiritual bride.

CHAPTER 2

A GOOD MAN
IS HARD TO FIND

"Go up and down
the streets of Jerusalem,
look around and consider,
search through her squares.
If you can find but one person
who deals honestly
and seeks the truth,
I will forgive this city."

JEREMIAH 5:1

God gives Jeremiah a chance to save his civilization. All he needs to find is one righteous person. Just one. Not one hundred, or fifty, or ten, or even two. Jeremiah is not looking for "a few good men;" he's looking for only one.

This is the offer God makes to his prophet:

"If you can find but one person
who deals honestly and seeks the truth,
I will forgive this city." (5:1b)

The challenge is to find a plain-dealer, just one citizen who can be trusted. For the sake of one person of real integrity, God will forgive the sins of the entire city.

According to the bargain, Jeremiah can take as long as he wants to look. And he has the whole city of Jerusalem to choose from:

> *"Go up and down the streets of Jerusalem,*
> *look around and consider,*
> *search through her squares."* (5:1a)

Jeremiah may scour the streets of the capital to find one righteous person. He starts with the common people, the regular folks, the "poor," as they are called (5:4). He seems to be cruising the right neighborhood, because he overhears plenty of religious jargon. "As surely as the LORD lives," they say (5:2). Among people who give lip service to God, a prophet might expect to find at least one good person.

Although the common people do have God's name on their lips, they do not have his glory on their minds. They have little respect for the Almighty:

> *"The house of Israel and the house of Judah*
> *have been utterly unfaithful to me,"*
> *declares the LORD.*
> *They have lied about the LORD;*
> *they said, "He will do nothing!*
> *No harm will come to us;*
> *we will never see sword or famine."* (5:11-12)

These poor people are in spiritual denial. They doubt that God judges sin or that he rules in history. For all their religious talk, they refuse to follow God. Their worship is false because they do not give glory to God in their hearts. By "swearing falsely" (5:2), they commit perjury when they worship.[1] This is a strong warning for anyone who claims to worship God.

Whenever hymns are mumbled or prayers are mindlessly repeated, perjury is committed in God's house.

As Jeremiah walks the streets of Jerusalem, he finds many people who have endured suffering. They have been struck down and crushed by the hardships of life. Among people who have endured such adversity, he might expect to find someone who fears God. Or someone who has learned obedience through suffering. Surely Jeremiah can find at least one!

Sadly, suffering has not produced character among the common folk:

> *O LORD, do not your eyes look for truth?*
> *You struck them, but they felt no pain;*
> *you crushed them, but they refused correction.*
> *They made their faces harder than stone*
> *and refused to repent.* (5:3)

They are callous, stubborn, and obstinate. They are men and women of steel. Their suffering has not produced godliness because they are immune to pain. They will not receive correction. Even after all Jeremiah's warnings, they refuse to repent.

Jeremiah begins to realize he is not getting anywhere in his search, so he changes his strategy. Perhaps he has been looking in all the wrong places. He has been looking low; now he will look high:

> *I thought, "These are only the poor;*
> *they are foolish,*
> *for they do not know the way of the LORD,*
> *the requirements of their God.*
> *So I will go to the leaders*
> *and speak to them." (5:4-5a)*

"What do you expect from the poor," Jeremiah says to himself. "They cannot read the Bible. They have not studied theology. They are sinning out of ignorance."

So Jeremiah goes to the high-rent district, where the priests and politicians live. After all, the religious leaders have been to seminary. They can read Torah. "Surely they know the way of the LORD, the requirements of their God!" (5:5b).

Not so. "With one accord they too had broken off the yoke and torn off the bonds" (5:5c). Jeremiah compares the cultural elite to dumb oxen who have shattered their yokes. The image captures their willful disobedience. They have not sinned out of ignorance like regular folks; they have sinned in defiance of the Word of God. Since they have broken free from divine authority, they are doubly culpable.

Jeremiah still needs to find one good man to save his city. Where else can he look? Not among the children. They, too, have forsaken the living God. "Why should I forgive you? Your children have forsaken me and sworn by gods that are not gods" (5:7a). They are worshiping the gods of the lower case, not God with a capital *G*. But lower-case gods are no gods at all. As Os Guinness shows in his book, there is *No God But God*.[2]

As a result, Jeremiah cannot find even one righteous child. Nor can he find a righteous adult, for they are busy committing religious adultery. "I supplied all their needs, yet they committed adultery and thronged to the houses of prostitutes" (5:7b). Like most good preachers, Jeremiah often repeats himself. Here he gives another reminder that although his people are married to the living God, they have been lavishing their affection on dead idols. As we noted in the first chapter, this adultery may have been literal as well as figurative, since many ancient religions—like Baal worship—included temple prostitution.

In this case, the people of Jerusalem "thronged to the houses of prostitutes" (5:7b). The word for thronging (*yitgodadu*) is a word for organizing an army into ranks and files. God's people are lining up to worship idols. Anyone who worships at the temples of the false gods will have to take a number.

Jeremiah goes so far as to once again compare the people of God to wild animals in heat (cf. 2:23-25). In their desperation to commit spiritual adultery, they are like "lusty stallions, each neighing for another man's wife" (5:8). Judah was a sex-crazed society, saturated with sexual immorality.

Not that they are deprived. God has given them everything they need. They are well-supplied (5:7) and "well-fed" (5:8). But instead of praising God for their affluence, they have turned to sexual sin. Jeremiah's Jerusalem is much like the pagan West, a culture one scholar has termed a "pornotopia."[3] All Jeremiah needs is one righteous person, but he will not find such a person among the wild broncos of Judah.

What about the preachers? Jeremiah offers a glimpse of the spiritual condition of his colleagues in ministry:

> "The prophets are but wind
> and the word is not in them;
> so let what they say be done to them." (5:13)

Prophets ought to speak the Word of God, but the only thing coming from these prophets is hot air. This is bitterly ironic because the word for wind is the same as the word for spirit (*ruach*). The prophets ought to be filled with the Spirit, but they are just windbags.

NOT EVEN ONE

All Jeremiah needs is one good man, but he is zero-for-Jerusalem. He cannot find so much as one righteous person among the poor, the leaders, the children, the adults, or the prophets.

The futility of Jeremiah's quest echoes Abraham's argument with God over the fate of Sodom (Gen. 18:16-33). Sodom was such a wicked city God planned to destroy it. But Abraham was unwilling to write the city off, so he bartered with God for its salvation. He started by getting God to agree to spare Sodom for the sake of fifty righteous people. The more he thought about it, however, the more impossible finding fifty honest pagans seemed. Gradually he worked God down to forty, down to twenty, and finally down to just ten righteous souls. God said, "For the sake of ten, I will not destroy it" (Gen. 18:32).

The sins of Sodom are well-known and often condemned, especially its homosexual sins. What Jeremiah has discovered, however, is that Jerusalem has become New Sodom. Salemites are no more righteous than Sodomites. Like Abraham before him, Jeremiah is unable to answer God's challenge to find the righteous among the wicked.

Jeremiah's search would have been equally futile if he had walked up and down the streets of my adopted city, Philadelphia. He would have had as much trouble finding one good person in the luxury apartments on Rittenhouse Square or among the tourists at Independence Mall. He would have found hatred and intolerance in Bridesburg and Gray's Ferry. He would have found drugs and violence in the Badlands of North Philly. Up on Society Hill he would have found selfishness and greed.

The search would be every bit as disappointing if Jeremiah walked all the towns and cities of the United States. He would have as much trouble finding a righteous person in Washington, or Peoria, or Kalamazoo. Could he have found truth among our journalists, honesty among our politicians, generosity among our businessmen, integrity among our clergy, or love within our families?

Indeed, Jeremiah's quest would have been equally hopeless if he had walked all the pages of human history. Where and when could he have found one person to be righteous for the people? If Jeremiah had lived for 3,000 years he would have had ample time to pace the streets of humanity, searching for "one person who deals honestly and seeks the truth."

He could have investigated the Vandals who sacked Rome. He could have taken a survey among the serfs of the Middle Ages. He could have searched through the kingdoms of Africa and lived among the emperors of China. He could have hunted buffalo with the Plains Indians and sipped tea with the Victorians. He could have observed the moral habits of the Eskimo, or even examined the members of your local church. But he would still be looking for one good person, righteous to the core, without any dissemblance or falsehood.

Would he have found anything different if he had knocked at your door?

Anyone who has ever looked for a perfectly good person has reached the same verdict. The philosophy major who wrote Ecclesiastes searched high and low and concluded that "there is not a righteous man on earth who does what is right and never sins" (Eccl. 7:20). The apostle Paul put it like this, loosely quoting King David:

> *What shall we conclude then? Are we any better?*
> *Not at all! . . . As it is written:*
> *"There is no one righteous, not even one;*
>   *there is no one who understands,*
>   *no one who seeks God.*
> *All have turned away,*
>   *they have together become worthless;*
>   *there is no one who does good,*
>   *not even one." (Rom. 3:9-12; cf. Ps. 14:1-3)*

This is one aspect of the doctrine of total depravity. The Bible does not teach that every human being is as bad as can be. But it does teach that every aspect of every person has been corrupted by sin. Bodies perform sinful acts and minds think sinful thoughts. The understanding, the heart, the will, and the imagi-

nation are all corrupted by sin. To paraphrase the title of an auto-
biography by Dennis Rodman of the Chicago Bulls basketball
team, we are as "Bad as We Wanna Be."

Depravity is total because it affects the whole person. It is
also total because it affects the whole of humanity. Total depravity is the one biblical doctrine that has been proven by every era
of human history. Even the pagan philosophers recognized the
sinfulness of the human race, although they could not fully
explain it. Diogenes the Cynic (fl.c. 350 B.C.) carried a lantern by
daylight, looking for one honest person. He failed in his quest.

Like Diogenes, Jeremiah received a lesson in total depravity.
The longer he walked the streets of Jerusalem, the clearer the lesson became: There is none righteous, no, not one.

THE WAGES OF SIN IS DEATH

If there is "no one righteous, not even one," then what will
become of the human race? Paul answers that question as well:
"The wages of sin is death" (Rom. 6:23). The *Catechism for
Young Children* puts the same truth slightly differently: Every sin
deserves "the wrath and curse of God" (Q & A 31). Total
depravity leads to total destruction.

Even someone who does not believe in God must admit that
sin deserves to be punished. God's moral law is imprinted on the
conscience. *Time* magazine once ran a story about the vile things
mass murderer Richard Speck did while he was in prison. Among
other things, he managed to star in his own pornographic video.
A caption for the story read, "The Wages of Sin Is . . ."
Underneath the caption was this quotation from Speck's video:
"If they only knew how much fun I was having in here, they
would turn me loose."[4] The caption was intended to provoke
outrage. The reason it had such an effect is because every human
being has an inherent sense of justice. Whatever the wages of sin
may be, they cannot include goofing off in jail.

Jeremiah teaches that the proper wages of sin is divine judgment. Already he has observed the leaders of Judah breaking free from God's yoke. Now he explains what happens to domesticated oxen when they leave the farm and roam free:

> *Therefore a lion from the forest will attack them,*
> *a wolf from the desert will ravage them,*
> *a leopard will lie in wait near their towns*
> *   to tear to pieces any who venture out,*
> *for their rebellion is great*
> *   and their backslidings many.* (Jer. 5:6)

Like a wounded cow, Judah will be stalked by one predator after another. A lion will attack from the forest, a wolf will ravage from the desert and leopards will lie in wait in suburbia.

The judgment continues with another image. Israel was planted to be a "choice vine" bearing good grapes for God (cf. 2:21), but now the vine is to be plucked:

> *"Go through her vineyards and ravage them,*
> *   but do not destroy them completely.*
> *Strip off her branches,*
> *   for these people do not belong to the LORD."* (5:10)

Then God's people are compared to kindling:

> *"Because the people have spoken these words,*
> *I will make my words in your mouth a fire*
> *and these people the wood it consumes."* (5:14)

The words of judgment Jeremiah speaks will be like consuming fire.

This language about wild animals, vines, and fire is metaphorical. What really will happen is that some unidentified foreign army will attack Jerusalem:

> *"O house of Israel," declares the* LORD,
>   *"I am bringing a distant nation against you—*
> *an ancient and enduring nation,*
>   *a people whose language you do not know,*
>   *whose speech you do not understand."* (5:15)

This prophecy refers to the Scythians, the Assyrians, or perhaps the Babylonians. In any case, the enemy will speak a foreign language, which will add to the terror of being defeated.

There is a terrifying scene in the movie *Platoon* in which an American military outpost is attacked by the Viet Cong at night. The outpost screams for help and maintains radio contact with headquarters. But when the Viet Cong win the skirmish, all the commander hears through his headset back at headquarters is soldiers chattering in Vietnamese. The battle has been lost, and an alien tongue adds to the horror of conquest.

Jeremiah speaks of an army so strong that even its wimps are bullies: "All of them are mighty warriors" (5:16). A three-year-old football fan once asked me about the New York Giants. He said, "But, Dad, if they're *giants,* then nobody could tackle them because they'd be too big!" That is what Judah's enemy will be like: every last man a giant, much too big to tackle.

By the time these voracious warriors are finished, they will have swallowed Judah whole:

> *"They will devour your harvests and food,*
>   *devour your sons and daughters;*
> *they will devour your flocks and herds,*
>   *devour your vines and fig trees."* (5:17a)

The next sentence is especially foreboding. "With the sword they will destroy the fortified cities in which you trust" (5:17b). The truth of this verse has been confirmed by archaeology. As William Foxwell Albright concluded concerning Israel's eventual destruction, "Many towns were destroyed at the beginning of the sixth century B.C. and never again occupied. . . . Others were destroyed and reoccupied after a long period of abandonment."[5] The wages of sin is death.

By the grace of God, some of the people of Judah will escape. A few grapes will be left on the vine (5:10). But even their future looks bleak. Once they have been carried off into exile, they will wonder why all these terrible things have happened to them. Their children, especially, will wonder what they have done to deserve such misfortune. God has a good answer:

> "And when the people ask,
> 'Why has the LORD our God done all this to us?'
>   you will tell them,
> 'As you have forsaken me and served foreign gods
>   in your own land,
>   so now you will serve foreigners
>   in a land not your own.'" (5:19)

God could hardly be any more fair! The people of Jerusalem have been worshiping foreign gods all along. What could be more appropriate than sending them to a place where they can serve those gods to their hearts' content?

Be careful what you desire: God might grant it!

THE RIGHTEOUS ONE

This is a good place to summarize the condition of Jerusalem as presented in the fifth chapter of Jeremiah. God will forgive the sins of the city if his prophet can find one honest, righteous, and truthful person left in it. But Jeremiah cannot find a single one. As a result, the people of Jerusalem are about to receive the wages of sin through divine judgment.

This is not just the condition of Jerusalem. It is the condition of the entire human race. There is no one righteous, not even one.

The wages of sin is death. If you belong to the human race, it is your condition as well.

If only the good man Jeremiah was looking for could be found! If only one man could be found who is honest in all his dealings, and who seeks the truth. If only one man could be found to be righteous for the people. If only that one man could be found, a man of such perfect integrity that he could turn away the wrath of God.

There is that man, Jesus Christ. What about him? Can he meet Jeremiah's conditions?

Jeremiah was told to look for a man "who deals honestly." Jesus Christ was straightforward in all his dealings. He gave an honest presentation of his deity, performing miracles to prove his divine power over creation. Jesus Christ dealt honestly with his disciples, not hiding from them the necessity of his own sufferings and death. Jesus Christ also dealt honestly with sinners, like the woman at the well (John 4), exposing their secrets and inviting them to trust in him. And Jesus Christ dealt honestly with his enemies, like the Pharisees, confronting the enmity in their hearts. There was nothing false or deceptive in anything Jesus said or did.

Jeremiah was told to look for a man "who seeks the truth." Jesus Christ not only sought the truth, he *is* the Truth! At the beginning of his gospel, John says Jesus Christ came into the world "full of grace and truth" (John 1:14). That is truth with a capital *T*, the Truth of God himself. Thus, when the disciples wanted to know the way to eternal life, Jesus said, "I am the way and the truth and the life" (John 14:6). *7, Truth revealer!*

The challenge God gave to Jeremiah was answered in Jesus Christ. He is the one man, the plain-dealer, the truth-seeker, the righteous man for whose sake God can forgive his people.

However, in order to achieve this forgiveness, it was necessary for Jesus Christ to die on the cross. Atonement had to be offered for the sins of God's people. Jeremiah's prophecy seems to recognize this need. "Should I not avenge myself on such a nation as this?" the Lord asked Judah (Jer. 5:9). "Why should I forgive you?" (5:7). Or, more accurately, "How *can* I forgive you?" This is the basic problem of salvation: How can God be just *and* justify the ungodly? (Rom. 3:26)

Only like this. Only if one perfect man, the God-and-man, would offer himself as a perfect sacrifice for sin. Such a man would be righteous, not only for himself, but also for others. Then God the Father would be able to forgive his people for their sins.

This is why the New Testament writers take great pains to prove that Jesus Christ is the one person who could and who did atone for all the sins of God's people. In Mark's gospel it is a demon who recognizes Jesus Christ, crying out, "I know who you are—the Holy One of God!" (Mark 1:24). In the book of Acts, Peter calls Jesus "the Holy and Righteous One" (Acts 3:14), while Stephen calls him "the Righteous One" (Acts 7:52; cf. 22:14). John says the same thing in his first epistle: "We have one who speaks to the Father in our defense—Jesus Christ, the Righteous One. He is the atoning sacrifice for our sins" (1 John 2:1-2a).

In John's gospel it is Caiaphas who testifies that Jesus is the answer to Jeremiah's quest. Caiaphas, who served as high priest in Jerusalem, was no friend of Jesus. Yet this is what he said, by the Holy Spirit: "It is better for you that one man die for the people than that the whole nation perish" (John 11:50). Exactly what Jeremiah was looking for: *one man* to save the nation from perishing! That one man is Jesus Christ, who died for the sins of his people so that they might not perish, but have everlasting life (John 3:16).

The apostle Paul said the same thing. He was "convinced that one died for all" (2 Cor. 5:14). He compared the death that came through Adam with the life that comes through Christ:

> For if the many died by the trespass of the one man [Adam], how much more did God's grace and the gift that came by the grace of the one man, Jesus Christ, overflow to the many! . . .

How much more will those who receive God's abundant pro-
vision of grace and of the gift of righteousness reign in life
through the one man, Jesus Christ. . . . The result of one act of
righteousness was justification that brings life for all men. For
just as through the disobedience of the one man [Adam] the
many were made sinners, so also through the obedience of the
one man [Christ] the many will be made righteous. (Rom. 5:15,
17-19)

Through the grace, the life, the righteous act, and the obedience of the one man, justifying grace comes to many.

Look as long as you like, there is no other answer to
Jeremiah's quest. God sent his own Son, Jesus Christ, the
Righteous One, to save the city. A Good Man is hard to find. But
not impossible.

CHAPTER 3

AT THE

CROSSROADS

"Stand at the crossroads and look;
ask for the ancient paths,
ask where the good way is, and walk in it,
and you will find rest for your souls.
But you said, 'We will not walk in it.'"

JEREMIAH 6:16

In his first inaugural address, President Franklin Delano Roosevelt (1882-1945) admitted that the United States of America had lost its way. "We don't know where we are going," he said, "but we are on our way."[1]

Roosevelt was right. We didn't know where we were going. At least, that is the conclusion Harvard scholar Oscar Handlin reached in a remarkable 1996 article called, "The Unmarked Way":

At some point, midway into the twentieth century, Europeans and Americans discovered that they had lost all sense of direction. Formerly, familiar markers along the way had guided their personal and social lives from birth to maturity to death. Now, disoriented, they no longer trusted the guideposts and groped in bewilderment toward an unimagined destination. Wandering in the dark, men and women in all Western societies, stumbling blindly along, strained unavailingly for glimpses of recognizable landmarks.[2]

Jeremiah could have said the same about his times. People had lost all sense of direction. They were disoriented. They groped in bewilderment and wandered in the dark. They needed a landmark, so Jeremiah gave them one:

> "Stand at the crossroads and look;
>   ask for the ancient paths,
>   ask where the good way is, and walk in it,
>   and you will find rest for your souls." (6:16)

This is a verse for people who have come to the crossroads and do not know which way to turn.

A FORK IN THE ROAD

The first thing to do is recognize the crossroads for what it is. Look around. Get your bearings. You have come to a fork in the road.

The people of God often find themselves at the crossroads. The children of Israel were at a crossroads when they gathered at Shechem. Joshua was about to die, so he said:

> "Now fear the LORD and serve him with all faithfulness. Throw away the gods your forefathers worshiped beyond the River and in Egypt, and serve the LORD. But if serving the LORD seems undesirable to you, then choose for yourselves this day whom you will serve, whether the gods your forefathers served beyond the River, or the gods of the Amorites, in whose land you are living. But as for me and my household, we will serve the LORD." (Josh. 24:14-15)

The people of God were at a crossroads when Elijah confronted the prophets of Baal on Mount Carmel. It was the same crossroads, offering the same two choices: God's way or the highway. Elijah said, "How long will you waver between two opinions? If the LORD is God, follow him; but if Baal is God, follow him" (1 Kings 18:21).

Western civilization now stands at the crossroads. We have started down the road to destruction, perhaps, but the way of life still stretches out before us. The ethical dilemmas we face show that we are at the crossroads. Will we cherish the lives of the innocent, or will we permit abortion on demand? Will we protect the lives of the defenseless, or will we allow involuntary euthanasia? Will we preserve the sanctity of marriage, or will we tolerate no-fault divorce and homosexual unions? Will we love the true and the beautiful, or will we gaze upon images of sex and violence? These are the questions a culture faces at the crossroads.

The evangelical church is also standing at the crossroads. Will we glorify God in our worship, or will we entertain ourselves? Will we bear witness to the law of God and the grace of the Gospel, or will we tone down our message so as not to offend anyone? Will we expound the eternal Word of God, or will we seek some new revelation? Will we defend the doctrine of justification by faith alone, or will we add works to grace? These are the questions a church faces when it stands at the crossroads.

Perhaps you are at a personal crossroads. Some Christians wonder what God wants them to do with their lives. Others contemplate a change of career, or the pursuit of a new educational opportunity, or the possibility of marriage, or a change of ministry within the church. Still others wrestle with deep spiritual questions, wondering who Jesus Christ is or if the Bible is really true.

The thing to do at such times is to recognize that you are standing at the crossroads. Two roads stretch before you. You can go in only one of two directions. Either you can keep going the way you have been going, or you can go down a different road altogether. Your destiny depends upon which road you take.

ON THE BEATEN TRACK

The second step is to ask for directions. When a nation, a church or an individual comes to a crossroads, it helps to have good road signs, good directions, or a good map. Jeremiah tells what kind of directions to get: "Ask for the ancient paths," he says. "Ask where the good way is" (Jer. 6:16).

In a paved society it is hard to understand what Jeremiah means. For automobiles, newly-paved roads are best, not old roads full of potholes. But in Jeremiah's day, people liked to travel on ancient pathways. Pedestrians wanted to follow a well-established route. In the wilderness, it is best to walk on a well-beaten path that has been trampled by many feet.

When Jeremiah says to "ask for the ancient paths," he is not suggesting living in the past. He is not being nostalgic. He is not proposing "that old-time religion."

There is too much talk these days about the alleged Christian faith of America's founding fathers. There is also overmuch talk about the glories of the Reformation. Some Christians pine away for some golden age of the historical church. But the Bible counsels against longing for the good old days. The philosopher warns, "Do not say, 'Why were the old days better than these?'" (Eccl. 7:10).

Jeremiah would have agreed with the philosopher. He is not telling God's people to live in the past. Instead, he is telling us to walk, here and now, according to the Word of God. The ancient path is the biblical path. The good way is the way marked out in the Scriptures. The Lord goes on to explain that the problem with the people of Jerusalem is that "they have not listened to my words and have rejected my law" (Jer. 6:19). In other words, they had made a bad choice back at the crossroads. And the reason they made a bad choice is that they rejected God's Word.

The people of God did exactly the opposite of what the

psalmist recommends. Psalm 119, the longest chapter in the Bible, is all about walking in the ancient way of God's Word. It starts out like this: "Blessed are they whose ways are blameless, who walk according to the law of the LORD" (Ps. 119:1).

Staying on track in life means going down the biblical path. The psalmist loved, read, meditated on, and prayed through God's Word. As he did all those things, he discovered that the Bible is like a smooth pathway for a difficult journey.

The psalmist often compares the Word of God to a pathway. "I run in the path of your commands, for you have set my heart free" (119:32). "Direct me in the path of your commands, for there I find delight" (119:35). "I have considered my ways and have turned my steps to your statutes" (119:59). "I gain understanding from your precepts; therefore I hate every wrong path" (119:104). "Your word is a lamp to my feet and a light for my path" (119:105). "Direct my footsteps according to your word" (119:133). Even in the very last verse of the psalm (v. 176), when the psalmist confesses that he has strayed like a lost sheep, the only reason he knows he has gone down the wrong road is that he has not forgotten God's commands.

The ancient path, the good way, is the Bible. Jeremiah's advice for people at the crossroads is to walk in the ancient path of biblical faith.

There is another way to interpret the ancient path and the good way. Jeremiah may be speaking, not only about the Bible, but also about sound theology in the history of the church. Other Christians have walked down the ancient path of the Bible, and they can show us the way.

Christians can learn from the past without living in the past. The evangelical church of the twenty-first century (should the Lord tarry) will live in post-Christian times. It cannot repeat the experiences of the Early Church Fathers, or the Reformers, or the Puritans, or anyone else in church history. But wherever Christians have followed in the footsteps of Christ, their footsteps should be followed. This is one good reason to recite the ancient creeds of the church. They represent what all Christians, everywhere, have always believed about God the Father, God the Son, and God the Holy Spirit.

It is possible to trace a straight pathway from the prophets and apostles to Augustine of Hippo, to Martin Luther, to John Calvin, to the Puritans, to the defenders of the faith in modern times. These are the theologians of the church who brought themselves under the authority of God's Word and testified to the sovereignty of God's grace in salvation. They maintained the glory of God as their chief end, the Scriptures of the Old and New Testaments as their only authority, and the righteousness of Christ received by faith as their only hope. Anyone who follows them, as they followed Scripture, has found the good way.

When the great evangelical theologian Charles Hodge (1797-1878) was named a full professor at Princeton Seminary in 1872, he testified that he was "not afraid to say that a new idea never originated in this Seminary."[3] Hodge did not mean that he could not think for himself; he was one of the leading intellects of his day. What he meant was that he wanted to be sound in his theology. He knew that sound theology does not go off in new directions. Hodge was not interested in being an innovator. He wanted to follow the ancient path, the good way.

Theological orthodoxy sounds old-fashioned. It seems out-of-date or even obsolete to some. But sound theology is like fine wine: It gets better with age. Jesus said, "No one after drinking old wine wants the new, for he says, 'The old is better'" (Luke 5:39). For novelty, go to the church that follows the latest fad. But novelty is the enemy of orthodoxy. It is much better to go where the eternal Word of God is preached and freshly applied to contemporary culture and the living church.

HE IS THE WAY

The ancient path, the good way, is the teaching of Scripture. It is orthodox theology. And it is also Jesus Christ. Those who seek the ancient path and the good way are seeking for Jesus Christ.

Jesus told his disciples he was going to his Father's house to prepare a place for them (John 14:1-2). He promised he would come back to take them there (14:3-4). He also told them they knew the pathway to the place where he was going (14:4). But the disciples were confused. They were not quite sure what Jesus was talking about. Frankly, they *didn't* know the way.

They could sense they were standing at a crossroads, however, and they knew they needed better directions. "Thomas said to him, 'Lord, we don't know where you are going, so how can we know the way?' Jesus answered, 'I am the way and the truth and the life. No one comes to the Father except through me'" (14:5-6).

Jesus Christ *is* the way. He is the ancient way and the good way. And he is the only way. Jesus is the only way to God, the only way to salvation and the only way to eternal life.

Jesus Christ is also the peaceful way. There is one place in the New Testament where Jesus seems to quote from Jeremiah 6:16. Jeremiah promised rest for the soul. Jesus said:

> *"Come to me, all you who are weary and burdened, and I will give you rest. Take my yoke upon you and learn from me, for I am gentle and humble in heart, and you will find rest for your souls."* (Matt. 11:28-29)

Those who walk in the ancient path and the good way find rest for their souls, which is exactly what people find when they come to Jesus Christ. He is the ancient, good, restful, and peaceful way. In Christ there is rest for the soul. If you are standing at a crossroads—culturally, ecclesiastically, or personally—what you need is biblical teaching, sound theology, and a personal relationship with Christ.

THE OBSTACLE COURSE

What happens to those who go down the other road? Jeremiah looks a little way down that road in the rest of chapter 6. It seems broad and easy, but it is a foolish route to take.

The state of Israel seemed to be at a crossroads in the spring of 1996, when a new Prime Minister was elected. Israelis were asked to choose between Shimon Peres, who offered peace, and Benjamin Netanyahu, who promised security. *Time* magazine said this about the importance of their choice:

> Sometimes statesmen stumble blindly over an epochal crossroads they do not know is there. Others are given the chance to see the fork in the road ahead and decide deliberately which way to go. Folly, wrote historian Barbara Tuchman, is when leaders knowingly choose the wrong path.[4]

True, isn't it? Folly is when people knowingly choose the wrong path. Here is a historical example:

> *"Stand at the crossroads and look;*
>   *ask for the ancient paths,*
> *ask where the good way is, and walk in it,*
>   *and you will find rest for your souls.*
>   *But you said, 'We will not walk in it.'"* (Jer. 6:16)

This is one of those biblical passages where one scratches one's head and says, "What are these people thinking?" The good and peaceful way is set before them, but they want nothing to do with it.

God placed Jerusalem at the crossroads. He put up road signs to show them which way to go. They were marked with a directional arrow and they read, "HERE, GO THIS WAY." God even handed them a road map in case they got lost, but they still insisted on taking the wrong road.

So God offered them even more help:

> *"I appointed watchmen over you and said,*
> *'Listen to the sound of the trumpet!'*
> *But you said, 'We will not listen.'"* (6:17)

The watchmen were the prophets—like Isaiah and Jeremiah—who warned Israel to leave their idols and return to God. But God's people would not listen, even when the trumpets of prophecy were blaring in their ears.

So God summons the nations and the earth itself into his cosmic jury box to be witnesses to their folly:

> *"Therefore hear, O nations;*
> *observe, O witnesses,*
> *what will happen to them.*
> *Hear, O earth:*
> *I am bringing disaster on this people,*
> *the fruit of their schemes,*
> *because they have not listened to my words*
> *and have rejected my law."* (6:18-19; cf. Deut. 30:19-20)

God filed for divorce back in chapter 2. Now he seems to render his final verdict. Disaster will fall on God's people for refusing to walk in the good path.

Why have God's people gone the wrong way? The next verse seems to give some insight into the nature of their sin:

> *"What do I care about incense from Sheba*
> *or sweet calamus from a distant land?*
> *Your burnt offerings are not acceptable;*
> *your sacrifices do not please me."* (6:20)

Some commentators conclude that Jeremiah was opposed to the Old Testament system of temple sacrifices.[5] They see contradictions between the regulations for sacrifices in the Torah and criticisms of temple worship in the prophets. But Jeremiah is not speaking against sacrifices themselves; he is only opposed to offering them with a wrong spirit.

The people of Jerusalem are very religious. They are becoming sophisticated, fashionable, up-to-date, and contemporary in their worship. Their services are lavish and ornate. They are importing exotic perfumes by camel—frankincense from Saudi Arabia and calamus from India—in order to spice up their worship. They are on an insatiable quest for the "latest thing." But their hearts have wandered far from God.

The ancient path is the simplicity of Word and Sacrament. The good way is simply the people of God meeting in the presence of God to pray, sing, break bread, and listen to God's Word (see Acts 2:42-47). Whenever buildings, instruments, sermons, or fellowship are used to entertain or fascinate rather than to glorify God, worship becomes unacceptable. The people of Jerusalem thought biblical worship was old-fashioned. They wanted to try something new-fangled. Yet John Guest writes this epitaph on their religious experiment: "Ritual performance perfumed with imported incense will never hide the stench of moral disobedience."[6]

So the Lord threatened to turn their new road into an obstacle course:

> *"I will put obstacles before this people.*
> *Fathers and sons alike will stumble over them;*
> *neighbors and friends will perish."* (Jer. 6:21)

It seemed like a good road at the beginning. It was wide and smooth. But the further they went, the narrower it became. The highway became a street. The street became a gravel road. The gravel road became a muddy track. Eventually, what started out as a Sunday drive turned into a steeplechase.

Some years ago I made a pilgrimage to Thomas Boston's church in the Scottish village of Ettrick. The longer I drove, the more difficult the road became, until I was dodging sheep on single-lane roads through the hills. This often happens when people get off the beaten track: There are obstacles in the road.

It is much safer to stay at home than to go down the wrong road. For those who refuse to go down the ancient path of the Bible and the good way of sound theology, even Jesus Christ becomes a stumbling block. The apostle Paul called Jesus Christ a "stumbling stone" (Rom. 9:32), a "stone that causes men to stumble and a rock that makes them fall" (9:33). If you refuse to walk in God's way, eventually the crucified and risen Christ will be your Judge, not your Savior.

If you have already gone down the wrong road, it is time to head back home. The English apologist Gilbert Keith Chesterton (1874-1936) had sound advice for people who lose their way:

> When you have lost your way quite hopelessly, the quickest thing is to go back along the road you know to the place from which you started. You may call it reaction, you may call it repetition, you may call it tiresome theory, but it is the quickest way out of the wood.

Jeremiah expresses the same idea in a single command: "Return!" (Jer. 3:12, 14). As you repent and obey, God will help you find your way to the ancient path and the good way.

CHAPTER 4

WHAT THE CHURCH NEEDS NOW IS REFORMATION!

"This is what the LORD Almighty . . . says: Reform your ways and your actions, and I will let you live in this place. Do not trust in deceptive words and say, 'This is the temple of the LORD, the temple of the LORD, the temple of the LORD!'"

JEREMIAH 7:3-4

In January 1519, something shocking happened at the Great Minster in Zurich. Everyone in the city was talking about it. One man said he was so excited he felt as if someone had grabbed him by his hair and lifted him out of his pew.

What was the cause of all this commotion? Simply this: Ulrich Zwingli (1484-1531), the new pastor of the church, was preaching the Word of God. At the first service in January, he opened his Bible to Matthew 1 and began to preach from the Scriptures. At the next service he picked up where he had left off in the gospel of Matthew and kept preaching. He did the same thing at the third service, and thereafter, verse by verse, chapter by chapter, book by book, right through the New Testament.

Then Zwingli started preaching through the Old Testament. Amazing! Unheard of! Soon men, women, and children came from all over Zurich to hear the minister explain the Bible in words they could understand.

Zwingli's systematic Bible exposition was the beginning of the Reformation in Switzerland. To this day, there is an inscription over the portal of the church that reads, "The Reformation of Huldrych Zwingli began here on January 1, 1519." Reformation begins with preaching God's Word.

THE TEMPLE SERMON

Long before Ulrich Zwingli, or Martin Luther, or John Calvin, there was a reformer named Jeremiah. If that great prophet were alive in these pagan times, he would do what the Protestant Reformers did: He would preach the Word of God. He would tell the evangelical church to mend its ways. He would teach that religious observance without moral obedience cannot save. He would say that what the church needs now is reformation.

Jeremiah 7 contains one of the great reformation sermons in the history of God's people. It is often called Jeremiah's Temple Sermon because God commanded him to "stand at the gate of the LORD's house and there proclaim this message" (7:2). One can imagine Jeremiah standing at one of the temple gates, watching the people of Israel come thronging up the temple steps to worship. Since his message is delivered to "all you people of Judah," it was most likely preached during one of the great religious festivals, such as Passover or the Feast of Tabernacles, when the whole nation came to Jerusalem to worship. The Lord wanted the Temple Sermon to get the widest possible hearing.

One thing that made the Temple Sermon a great sermon was that it was preached at a moment of historical destiny. The sermon is reprinted in chapter 26, with this additional detail: "Early in the reign of Jehoiakim son of Josiah king of Judah, this word came from the LORD" (26:1).

Jeremiah preached his sermon, therefore, at a time of national crisis. The people of Judah had lost hope in the power of political solutions to solve their problems. "While Josiah was king, Pharaoh Neco king of Egypt went up to the Euphrates River to help the king of Assyria. King Josiah marched out to meet him in battle, but Neco faced him and killed him at Megiddo" (2 Kings 23:29). Josiah, the great reforming king of Judah, was dead.

Now, after the light of Josiah's reformation, Judah is slipping back into spiritual darkness. Josiah's son Jehoahaz had only reigned in Jerusalem for three months before Pharaoh Neco carried him off to Egypt, where he died (2 Kings 23:31-34). Jehoiakim is on the throne, but who knows how long he will last? Judah is at another crossroads—a political and spiritual crossroads—as Jeremiah mounts the temple steps to preach.

The message he gives is not popular:

> As soon as Jeremiah finished telling all the people everything the LORD had commanded him to say, the priests, the prophets and all the people seized him and said, "You must die! Why do you prophesy in the LORD's name that this house will be like Shiloh and this city will be desolate and deserted?" . . . Then the priests and the prophets said to the officials and all the people, "This man should be sentenced to death because he has prophesied against this city. You have heard it with your own ears!" (Jer. 26:8-9, 11)

The religious establishment wants to wring Jeremiah's neck. This often happens to reformers. The same thing happened to Martin Luther (1483-1546) when he started to preach his reformation sermons. The Pope attacked Luther's preaching, calling him a wild boar, a serpent, and a "pestiferous virus."[1]

A FALSE HOPE

What is so pestiferous about Jeremiah's message?

The content of his Temple Sermon can be summarized: Religious observance without moral obedience cannot save. John Calvin put it like this: "Sacrifices are of no importance or value before God, unless those who offer them wholly devote themselves to God with a sincere heart."[2] It can be stated even more briefly: Those who seek justification without sanctification need reformation.

The first thing to understand about Jeremiah's message is that it is being delivered to a religiously observant people. Jeremiah is preaching to people who are on their way to the temple to offer sacrifices to God. They are wearing their Passover best, and they have their scrolls tucked under their arms.

Reformation always begins with the people of God. Reformation is something that starts in the church. It begins when God's own people are convicted of their sins and turn to God with new repentance, trust in God with new faith, and walk with God in new obedience. That kind of spiritual reformation always has an influence on the city, the society or the civilization. But it always starts in the hearts of God's people.

The people of Judah are in desperate need of reformation because they have put their trust in the outward trappings of religion. Their approach to theology—which could be called their "Temple Theology"—can be summarized like this: "This is the temple of the LORD, the temple of the LORD, the temple of the LORD." It is not a complicated theology. The people have taken their faith in the living God and have reduced it to trust in a building. They know enough not to put their trust in kings. After all, they have watched Josiah die in battle at Megiddo, and they have seen Jehoahaz being dragged down to Egypt. But still they believe that the temple in Jerusalem will keep them safe. They are putting their trust in the outward trappings of religion.

They are half right, which is the way false theology usually works. Most heresies are half made up of truth. It is the other half one has to worry about. In this case, the people know God has chosen Jerusalem to be his holy city. They know God promised he would never abandon his dwelling place. They know he will defend and save his city (Isa. 37:35). Each year, when they go up to worship at the temple in Jerusalem, they sing:

> For the LORD has chosen Zion,
>   he has desired it for his dwelling:
> "This is my resting place for ever and ever;
>   here I will sit enthroned,
>   for I have desired it." (Ps. 132:13-14)

The problem is that God's people think God's promise about the temple gives them the freedom to live immoral lives. The temple has become a superstition. They assume that as long they fulfill their religious obligations, they can do whatever they want with the rest of their lives.

Their Temple Theology has nothing to say about holy living. They assume God will never judge them for their sins, which is why Jeremiah tries to reason with them: "Look here, you are trusting in deceptive words that are worthless" (Jer. 7:8). They want faith without practice. They want covenant blessing without covenant obedience. They want to be justified without being sanctified.

What they are really doing is presuming upon divine election. They are assuming that because they are God's chosen people, living in God's chosen city, worshiping in God's chosen temple, no harm can ever come to them. But they are living in sin, which means they have never truly understood the marvel of God's grace.

That is a strong warning for anyone who has experienced God's sovereign grace, yet continues to live in sin. If you are unrepentant about lust, or about loving some worldly thing, or about bitterness, or about greed, or about any sin whatsoever, you are presuming upon God's grace. Know this: You cannot separate justification (God declaring you righteous) from sanctification (God making you righteous). If you have done so, what you need is reformation.

Jeremiah's message is also a strong warning to everyone who seeks to be justified before God by religious observance. Some put their trust in church attendance and say, "I go to church, I go to church, I go to church." Some put their trust in religious experience and say, "I'm born again, born again, born again." Some put their trust in a sacrament and say, "I've been baptized, baptized, baptized." Some put their trust in church affiliation and say, "I belong to an evangelical church, evangelical church, evangelical church." Others put their trust in religious duties and say, "I have daily devotions, daily devotions, daily devotions." Still others put their trust in some theological principle separated from a personal relationship with Jesus Christ. They say, "I believe in the doctrines of grace, the doctrines of grace, the doctrines of grace."

All these things are good in themselves. That is what is so dangerous about the temptation to put confidence in outward religion. There was absolutely nothing wrong with the temple in Jerusalem. The people of God were *supposed* to go there to worship. Nor is there anything wrong with going to church, being born again, being baptized, becoming a member of a particular church, having daily devotions, or believing the doctrines of grace. Not only is there nothing wrong with these things, all of them are positively necessary for growing in the Christian faith.

But do not put your trust in these things. Do not trust church attendance, or a conversion experience, or a sacrament, or church membership, or spiritual exercises for salvation. Instead, like the apostle Paul, "Worship by the Spirit of God . . . glory in Christ Jesus," and "put no confidence in the flesh" (Phil. 3:3).

Instead, trust in the righteousness that comes from God and is by faith in Jesus Christ (Phil. 3:9). Trust in Christ *alone* for salvation. He is all our hope and trust.

A LIFE OF SIN

That is half of the problem. God's people are trusting in superficial religiosity to save them. What about the other half?

Remember the message of Jeremiah's Temple Sermon: Religious observance without moral obedience cannot save. The other half of the problem is that God's people are not obedient. They are living sinful lives. They do not realize that moral integrity is more important to God than showing up at a house of worship on the Sabbath.

They say to God, "the temple, the temple, the temple." But God said to them, "if, if, if . . .": "*If* you really change your ways and your actions and deal with each other justly, *if* you do not oppress the alien, the fatherless or the widow and do not shed innocent blood in this place, and *if* you do not follow other gods to your own harm . . ." (Jer. 7:5-6).

This is a catalogue of the sins of God's people. A close look shows that they are violating virtually every one of the Ten Commandments (Ex. 20:1-17). The first commandment says to have no other gods before God. Well, they are following other gods (Jer. 7:9). The second commandment says not to make idols, but the people of Judah are burning incense to Baal. The third commandment says not to take the name of the Lord in vain, but they are profaning the house that bears God's name (7:10). The fourth commandment says to honor the Sabbath, but they are offering false worship on the day of worship. They are violating all the commandments that deal with one's relationship to God.

What about the commandments that govern human relationships? The fifth commandment gives honor to parents, but the people are neglecting their social responsibilities to the fatherless and the widow (7:6). Commandments six through nine say, "Do not murder, do not commit adultery, do not steal, and do not bear false witness." All these sins are mentioned in verse 9: "Will you steal and murder, commit adultery and perjury?" Run a finger down the list: Judah is rejecting everything God's law stands for.

All the commandments are being broken, but Jeremiah has a special concern for social justice. God's wants his nation to be a caring society, but they do not deal justly with one another. They do not take care of the disadvantaged. To learn how compassionate a society is, and how just, find out what happens to the underclass. How orphans, immigrants, and single-parent families are treated indicates how godly a society is.

A church can be tested using the same standard. How active is its concern for the homeless, the elderly, the disabled, or for broken families? What Jeremiah sees when he walks around Jerusalem is that people are not very concerned.

It is bad enough to commit all these sins, but what God's people have done is even worse. They have violated all God's commandments, and then they have gone to worship in God's house as if they have done nothing wrong. They think reformation has to do with Sabbath worship. They do not understand that reformation has to do with all of life. They think they can spend six days breaking all God's commandments as long as they spend one day singing Scripture songs and taking sermon notes. They think they can divorce worship from daily life.

Here is what God wants to know: Will they do all these things "and then come and stand before me in this house, which bears my Name, and say, 'We are safe'—safe to do all these detestable things?" (7:10). God's people are using God's temple as a safe house. They go out on crime sprees and then go back and use the temple for a hideout. They are wolves in sheep's clothing.

That is why the Lord says, "Has this house, which bears my

Name, become a den of robbers to you?" (7:11). Jesus said the same thing when he went to the temple. The people of Jerusalem used the temple courts as a place to do shady business. So Jesus threw over the tables of the money changers and said, "It is written, . . . 'My house will be called a house of prayer,' but you are making it a 'den of robbers'" (Matt. 21:13).

The people of Judah are operating on the assumption that God neither sees nor cares about what they do during the week. They think they can fool God by showing up for worship on the Sabbath and on the major holy days, and then go out and do whatever they want the rest of the time. They want to be justified without being sanctified.

They say you can fool some of the people some of the time, but God is no fool. Ever. His people can run back to their den of thieves, but they cannot hide, because God has them under constant surveillance: "I have been watching! declares the LORD" (Jer. 7:11). God is omniscient. He knows all things, which includes knowing when people walk into his house with dirty shoes.

A HISTORY LESSON

This is Jeremiah's message: Religious observance without moral obedience cannot save. What the church needs now is reformation.

What happens if a church or a nation refuses to mend its ways? Jeremiah often gives an answer to such questions. He tells what happens to those who will not follow God. This time he offers to take the people of God on a historical field trip: "Go now to the place in Shiloh" (7:12).

What is there to see at Shiloh? Not much. Shiloh is where the temple *used* to be, where, as God says, "I first made a dwelling for my Name" (7:12). Many years before, "the whole assembly of the Israelites gathered at Shiloh and set up the Tent of Meeting there" (Josh. 18:1). The Tent of Meeting was where the ark of the covenant was located, the ark that contained the earthly presence of Almighty God. The ark of God's presence stayed at Shiloh for many years. When Samuel went to serve Eli at the temple, for example, he did not go to Jerusalem, but to Shiloh (1 Sam. 1:3).

The ark of the covenant did not remain in Shiloh, however, because the people did not obey God. They carted the ark off to the battlefield to use it as a lucky charm against the Philistines. It was captured in battle, only to be returned when the Philistines discovered how dangerous it is to live in God's presence, as embodied in the ark (1 Sam. 4-6). The ark was then taken first to Beth Shemesh and then to Kiriath Jearim, where David later found it and brought it to Jerusalem (2 Sam. 6:2).

If the people of God in Jeremiah's day went to Shiloh, they would not find the house of God or the living presence of God, but only a pile of rubble. The archaeological evidence shows that Shiloh was destroyed twice over: once by the Philistines and once when the Assyrians carried the northern tribes into captivity (cf. Jer. 7:15).[3]

When Jeremiah tells the people of God to go to Shiloh, he is telling them to go to the place where God is not. Shiloh is the place where God once was and is no longer. As Asaph wrote,

> They angered [God] with their high places,
>   they aroused his jealousy with their idols.
> When God heard them, he was very angry;
>   he rejected Israel completely.
> He abandoned the tabernacle of Shiloh,
>   the tent he had set up among men. (Ps. 78:58-60)

Shiloh thus represents the absence and abandonment of God, with the end of his worship.

The people of Jerusalem think such a disaster will never happen to them. "We have the temple of the Lord, the temple of the Lord, the temple of the Lord," they say (cf. Jer. 7:4). They know it happened to Shiloh, but they do not realize it could happen to them as well. They know it happened to the liberals, but they do not think it could ever happen to conservatives. They remember all the time and energy they invested in repairing the temple—all the collections they took, all the stone they cut and all the timber they bought (2 Kings 22:3-7)—and they cannot imagine the temple ever being destroyed.

They are wrong. Religious observance without moral obedience cannot save. They put their confidence in the outward trappings of religion rather than in a living relationship with God himself.

The ruins of Shiloh stand as a warning to them, and also to us. There are Shilohs all around the post-Christian West. There are Shilohs, for example, in Oxford, England. Down the Cowley Road there is a large Methodist church where revival meetings used to be held; now it is a full-time bingo parlor. Down the Headington Road there is a Baptist church that has become an Islamic mosque.

There is a Shiloh in Cape May, New Jersey. The Admiral, an immense Christian conference center, used to dominate the Cape May skyline. But the Admiral has been destroyed. The property has been subdivided into housing lots.

There are dozens of Shilohs in Philadelphia. There is a Shiloh at 15th and Locust, where the old First Presbyterian Church used to stand. Now it is a parking garage. In other words, they "paved First Pres. and put up a parking lot"! Another Presbyterian church building still stands at 34th and Chestnut. It is not a church anymore, though—it has been converted into a Creative Motions Dance Studio.

There is a Shiloh at 22nd and Walnut, where an Episcopal church has been torn down and replaced by a Sunoco mini-mart. The steeple of the old church is visible only in the mural on the wall next to the store. The church has become a shadow in the city, nothing more than a reflection in a painted window on an urban wall.

There are Shilohs all around, like so many skeletons on the pilgrim road. They are places where God used to be worshiped in Spirit and in truth. They are places where praise was given to God in the name of Jesus Christ. They are places where the counsel of God was preached. But they are all places where God is worshiped no longer.

The Shilohs on the pagan landscape stand as a warning. They are a reminder that the living God does not dwell in a building made of human hands (Acts 17:24). No building, no church, no congregation has a permanent hold on his presence. The perseverance of God's people in any place depends upon God's grace. There is nothing sacred about buildings. Church structures provide no protection on the day of judgment.

On the other hand, there is a church in the city of Wenzhou in China that has abandoned its building but appears to be in no danger of becoming a Shiloh.

The Chinese government takes a dim view of religious devotion. So in the mid-1990s they commandeered a church building in Wenzhou and appointed one of their own officials to "pastor" the church. Talk about letting a wolf into the sheepfold! The church had a large congregation, more than a thousand members in all. They had built their church building with their own hands, but the government told them either to accept the new "pastor" or to leave the premises. The pastoral council decided to leave the church building with as many members as were willing to go. Within two days they divided the congregation into dozens of house churches. They needed dozens of homes because 900 members were willing to leave their building behind.

What they wanted, more than anything else, was the living presence of God in their worship. They did not say "Wenzhou Church, Wenzhou Church, Wenzhou Church." They had placed their confidence, not in the outward trappings of Christianity, but in Jesus Christ himself. They were unwilling to settle for anything less than the pure worship of God and the unhindered presentation of the Gospel. As long as they remain faithful to God, they will never become a Shiloh.

This is an example for the Western church, which has fallen on pagan times. What the church needs now is not building programs or new methods of church growth. What the church needs now is reformation.

CHAPTER 5

SOMETHING TO
BOAST ABOUT

"Let not the wise man boast of his wisdom
or the strong man boast of his strength
or the rich man boast of his riches,
but let him who boasts boast about this:
  that he understands and knows me,
that I am the LORD, who exercises kindness,
  justice and righteousness on earth,
  for in these I delight."

JEREMIAH 9:23-24

When I became a member of Tenth Presbyterian Church in Philadelphia, I received a booklet explaining my responsibilities as a church member. The first page featured a Bible verse written and signed by the pastor, Dr. James Montgomery Boice.

I later learned that Dr. Boice often chooses a verse appropriate for the new member's name, occupation, or spiritual condition. Here is the verse he chose for me:

"Let him who boasts boast about this:
  that he understands and knows me,
that I am the LORD, who exercises kindness,
  justice and righteousness on earth,
  for in these I delight." (Jer. 9:24)

On the occasion of my ordination to the pastoral ministry, my sister-in-law wrote to give me the same verses in a different translation:

> *"Let not the wise man glory in his wisdom,*
> *Let not the mighty man glory in his might,*
> *Nor let the rich man glory in his riches;*
> *But let him who glories glory in this,*
> *That he understands and knows Me,*
> *That I am the LORD, exercising lovingkindness,*
> *judgment, and righteousness in the earth.*
> *For in these I delight." (9:23-24; NKJV)*

I have not had the courage to ask either Dr. Boice or my sister-in-law why these verses seem so appropriate for me! Perhaps it is because I am boastful by nature. If so, then I receive these verses gladly, for they remind me not to boast about things that are nothing to boast about. Or perhaps this passage is suitable for me because it is my job to boast. I am a professional boaster, for to preach is to boast. And Jeremiah 9:23-24 gives a preacher—or any other Christian, for that matter—plenty to boast about.

THE GRIM REAPER

Because they are often sung or memorized, these verses are familiar to many Christians. Yet the place they occupy in Jeremiah's teaching is rarely considered. Calvin commented that,

> This is a remarkable passage, and often found in the mouth of men, as other notable sentences, which are known as proverbial sayings: but yet few rightly consider how these words are connected with the previous context.[1]

As Calvin well knew, the context of these verses is divine judgment. Jeremiah's invitation to boast comes in the middle of punishment for sin. Chapter after chapter, verse by verse, over and over again Jeremiah teaches the same lesson: God is a holy God who does not overlook sin, but brings sinners to judgment.

Jeremiah chapter 9 contains many righteous judgments. The God who once gave his people manna in the wilderness and water from the rock now offers them wormwood and gall: "See, I will make this people eat bitter food and drink poisoned water" (9:15). This prophesy is about a national calamity in the food and water supplies.

It is followed by a prophecy of exile: "I will scatter them among nations that neither they nor their fathers have known" (9:16). Prophecies of exile become more frequent as the Babylonians march closer and closer to Jerusalem. When judgment finally comes, the land will be destroyed. "We must leave our land," the people will lament, "because our houses are in ruins" (9:19b). The Babylonians will destroy Jerusalem's infrastructure.

They will also decrease Jerusalem's population. Jeremiah provides lyrics for a dirge. His song for the dead sends shivers up and down the spine, like a chilling passage from a Stephen King novel:

> *Death has climbed in through our windows*
> *and has entered our fortresses.* (9:21a)

This is death personified. Death is the Prowler who comes by night, the Stalker who peeks in the window, the Intruder who climbs into the house to commit murder. Death is the stealthy Assassin who penetrates the defenses and slips into the fortified castle. Or death is a Body Snatcher:

> *It has cut off the children from the streets*
> *and the young men from the public squares.* (9:21b)

Death even grabs kids off the playground. There is nowhere to run and nowhere to hide.

Worse still, death will treat the dead like so much garbage, denying them a proper burial:

> *"The dead bodies of men will lie*
> *like refuse on the open field,*
> *like cut grain behind the reaper,*
> *with no one to gather them."* (9:22)

This macabre massacre is well-illustrated in a painting by Winslow Homer. The painting shows a wide field of wheat against a blue horizon. In the foreground a man swings a scythe; dark cut grain is strewn all around him. The painting is not about farming, however; it is about war and death. It is evident from the farmer's garments that he has recently returned from fighting for the Union in the Civil War. The wheat he mows down before the blue horizon represents the destruction of the South.

Death is the Grim Reaper who leaves the dead bodies of men like cut grain in an open field. Henry Wadsworth Longfellow (1807-1882) described him like this:

> *There is a Reaper, whose name is Death,*
> *And, with his sickle keen,*
> *He reaps the bearded grain at a breath,*
> *And the flowers that grow between.*[2]

THE SCHOOL OF SADNESS

Jeremiah must have been disturbed by these images of death. He asks,

> *What man is wise enough to understand this? Who has been instructed by the LORD and can explain it? Why has the land been ruined and laid waste like a desert that no one can cross?* (9:12)

The answer is not hard to find. Death is the inevitable consequence of sin:

The LORD said, "It is because they have forsaken my law, which I set before them; they have not obeyed me or followed my law. Instead, they have followed the stubbornness of their hearts; they have followed the Baals, as their fathers taught them." (9:13-14)

God's people have received judgment the old-fashioned way: They earned it. The question is not, "What have these people done to deserve this?" The question is, "What *haven't* they done?" You name it, they have done it: idol worship, adultery, lying, child sacrifice, not praising God, prostitution, unfaithfulness, treachery, shady dealings, false preaching, not fearing God, covenant-breaking, violence, greed, not walking in God's way, hypocrisy, racism, murder, goddess worship, slander, and rejecting the Word of God. In a word, they are stubborn (9:14), which means to exhibit "a defiant attitude toward the Lord, a rejection of his law, a preference for other gods, and a refusal to repent."[3]

If these sins sound familiar it is because they are the sins of our own pagan times: adultery, dishonesty, godlessness, racism, goddess worship, and so on. Such sins call for lamentation, which is one of the chief duties of the Christian in declining times. Christians are to weep over the sins of the church, the transgressions of the nation, and the fearfulness of the judgment to come.

Jeremiah beckons the skillful wailing women to come in haste:

"Call for the wailing women to come;
*   send for the most skillful of them.*
Let them come quickly
*   and wail over us*
till our eyes overflow with tears
*   and water streams from our eyelids." (9:17-18)*

These women are mourners by occupation. They are real pros. "In the Middle East even today, on the occasion of deaths or calamities, mourning is carried out by professional women who follow the funeral bier uttering a high-pitched shriek."[4] Jeremiah invites the wailing women to let their tears flow into the eyes of their friends and neighbors so the whole nation can weep together.

Jerusalem will need as many mourners as she can get. Lamentation will become a growth industry: "Teach your daughters how to wail; teach one another a lament" (9:20). There will be plenty of job opportunities for professional wailing women. God may speak to the women because they are more given to tears, but these verses are not just for women. Every Christian is called to weep with those who weep (Rom. 12:15).

In these pagan times, Christians will need to rediscover the lost art of lamentation. In addition to teaching sons and daughters how to hate sin and fear its consequences, we must impress upon them the sadness of sin. As we pass a playground on the way to worship on the Lord's Day, my son may say, "Why aren't those guys going to church?" "Oh," I say, "it's a very sad thing, my son, but some people do not love the Lord. They do not know that Sunday morning is a time for worship and not for basketball." Or we see parents fighting with children at the shopping mall. Dysfunctional families are distressing to watch. The primary emotion they ought to evoke is sadness for sin.

If Jeremiah 9 is any indication, the Lord calls some Christians to a ministry of lamentation. He has called "some to be apostles, some to be prophets, some to be evangelists, and some to be pastors and teachers" (Eph. 4:11). Others exercise the gift of helps or intercession. But where are the wailing women and mourning men of the evangelical church? Francis Schaeffer reminds us that,

> With love we must face squarely the fact that our culture really is under the judgment of God. . . . We must proclaim the message with tears and give it with love. . . . It will not

do to say these things coldly. Jeremiah cried, and we must cry for the poor lost world, for we are all of one kind. . . . I *must* have tears for my kind.[5]

Who will lament the sins of the church, the transgressions of the nation, and the fearfulness of the judgment to come?

NOTHING TO BOAST ABOUT

It is just at this point—right in the context of sin, judgment, and lamentation—that Jeremiah warns about improper boasting:

> "*Let not the wise man boast of his wisdom*
> *or the strong man boast of his strength*
> *or the rich man boast of his riches.*" (Jer. 9:23)

It is in the face of divine judgment that wisdom, strength, and riches are nothing to boast about.

Wise people do love to boast about their wisdom. It starts early in elementary school: "I got a sticker on my paper; what did you get?" By the time some people get to college, their boasting is out of control. During my first term at Oxford I had the misfortune to walk behind two first-year students in the High Street. "So," said one Fresher to the other, "how's your arrogance coming along?"

Such boasting is not new. Back in the nineteenth century a scholar from Padua paid a visit to Oxford. He did not find any members of the university who knew everything, but he did find plenty of know-it-alls:

> Elsewhere I have asked a professor of astronomy some questions regarding anatomy, or botany, and he had the courage and honesty at once frankly to answer, "I do not know." But at Oxford it really seemed as if everybody considered himself equally bound to be universal, to know

everything, and to be able to give some sort of affirmative answer to every question, however foreign it might be to his ordinary and proper pursuits. There is so much wisdom in answering seasonably, "I do not know," that in a university which has been celebrated, and accounted most wise for nine or ten centuries, I thought for the credit of the place, I ought to get it once, at least, before I went away; so I tried hard, but I could never attain it. Why was this?[6]

The apostle Paul had a simple answer for the mystified academic from Padua: "Knowledge puffs up" (1 Cor. 8:1). Intellectual accomplishments feed the ego.

The wise person may boast of his or her wisdom, but a high I.Q. is nothing to boast about. Only God knows all things, and all wisdom comes from him. Whatever is good, true, wise, or beautiful is already known by God. Therefore, the best intellectual accomplishment is to think God's thoughts after him:

Where is the wise man? Where is the scholar? Where is the philosopher of this age? Has not God made foolish the wisdom of the world? . . . We preach Christ crucified: a stumbling block to Jews and foolishness to Gentiles, but to those whom God has called, both Jews and Greeks, Christ the power of God and the wisdom of God. For the foolishness of God is wiser than man's wisdom. (1 Cor. 1:20, 23-25)

To be truly wise, begin with the fear of the Lord (Prov. 1:7) and then seek the knowledge of God in the face of Jesus Christ (2 Cor. 4:6).

So much for the wise. What about the strong? Strong men, too, like to boast about their strength. Athletes are no longer content to score touchdowns, tackle quarterbacks, or make three-pointers. They want to strut, dance, taunt, jump into the crowd, and humiliate their opponents. Boxers and wrestlers spend as much time jawing as they spend working out. Back in the early seventies, when Muhammad Ali told everyone he was "the greatest," it was a novelty. Now everyone is doing it.

The strong man may boast in his strength, but a physique is nothing to boast about. For one thing, the strength of a man is not to be compared to the strength of God. The apostle Paul addressed this topic as well. In fact, he seems to have had Jeremiah 9 in mind when he wrote to the Corinthians. After saying that "the foolishness of God is wiser than man's wisdom," he goes on to say that "the weakness of God is stronger than man's strength" (1 Cor. 1:25). Furthermore, human strength, as weak as it is, diminishes with age. At the 1996 Olympics in Atlanta it was everything Muhammad Ali could do to stand in silence and lift the Olympic Torch.

The rich are as boastful as the wise and the strong. Jesus told the story of a rich man who had so many possessions he had no place to keep them:

> "Then he said, 'This is what I'll do. I will tear down my barns and build bigger ones, and there I will store all my grain and my goods. And I'll say to myself, "You have plenty of good things laid up for many years. Take life easy; eat, drink and be merry."'
>
> "But God said to him, 'You fool! This very night your life will be demanded from you. Then who will get what you have prepared for yourself?'" (Luke 12:18-20)

Jesus explained the point of the story: "This is how it will be with anyone who stores up things for himself but is not rich toward God" (12:21). In other words, you can't take it with you.

The Puritan Thomas Fuller pointed out the two basic problems with wealth: "Riches may leave us while we live, we must leave them when we die." Earthly riches are no lasting treasure.

Wisdom, strength, riches—these things are nothing to boast about. Neither is anything else apart from God himself. John Calvin explained:

Not only condemned in these words is the boasting of
human power, and the glorying in wisdom and in wealth,
but that men are wholly stripped of all the confidence they
place in themselves, or seek from the world, in order that
the knowledge of God alone may be deemed enough for
obtaining perfect happiness.[7]

You may be smart. You may be strong. You may be rich. But you
have nothing to boast about:

> *The race is not to the swift*
>   *or the battle to the strong,*
> *nor does food come to the wise*
>   *or wealth to the brilliant*
>   *or favor to the learned;*
> *but time and chance happen*
> *to them all.* (Eccl. 9:11)

Neither your mind nor your body can give ultimate security
in this life. Or the next.

Jeremiah discovered the same truths. Death and destruction
will overtake everyone who trusts in worldly wisdom, human
strength, or earthly treasure. When people are scattered among
the nations, houses lie in ruins, death climbs in through the window, and the Grim Reaper takes his sickle to the grain, then all
boasting must come to an end. The dead do not boast.

BOAST ABOUT THIS

The Christian, however, does have one thing to boast about:

> *"Let him who boasts boast about this:*
>   *that he understands and knows me,*
> *that I am the LORD, who exercises kindness,*
>   *justice and righteousness on earth,*
>   *for in these I delight."* (Jer. 9:24)

If you must boast—as all human beings must, because we were made to boast—then boast about the understanding and knowledge of God. Your boast is not that *you* understand and know God. The only reason you know God is because he has revealed himself through his Word and his world. But you may boast about God himself. The Christian's proper boast is in a Godward direction.

So boast about this, that God is the Lord who made heaven and earth, the Lord God of Abraham, Isaac, and Jacob. He is the Lord who met Moses at the burning bush and brought the children of Israel out of their bondage in Egypt. He is the Lord who helped Joshua conquer the Promised Land, and whom David praised when he said, "The LORD is my shepherd" (Ps. 23:1). He is the Lord who sent fire to consume Elijah's altar when all the people said, "The LORD—he is God! The LORD—he is God!" (1 Kings 18:39). And he is the same Lord who brought his people back from their captivity in Babylon.

To boast in the Lord is also to boast in Jesus Christ. A boast about the "Godness" of God is a boast about the lordship of Jesus Christ. The Lord God of the Old Testament is one and the same with God the Son in the New Testament:

> God exalted him to the highest place
>   and gave him the name that is above every name,
>   that at the name of Jesus every knee should bow,
>   in heaven and on earth and under the earth,
>   and every tongue confess that Jesus Christ is Lord,
>   to the glory of God the Father
>   (Phil. 2:9-11; cf. Isa. 45:22-25)

Now that *is* something to boast about. Jesus Christ is the risen Lord who must receive all praise, glory, and worship. The lordship of Jesus Christ is the Christian's best boast.

Since you, as a human being, will boast from time to time, boast also about this, that the Lord exercises kindness on earth (9:24). This "kindness" means more than being nice, like feeding the dog or helping a little old lady across the street. Kindness, or *chesed* in Hebrew, is so rich that it takes a half dozen English words to convey its meaning. It means covenant loyalty, steadfast love, unfailing devotion, and merciful affection. The King James and *New American Standard* versions translate it best as "lovingkindness." Kindness is the love of God expressed through Jesus Christ in the eternal covenant of God's grace.

God speaks of his kindness in the Ten Commandments when he promises to show "lovingkindness to thousands, to those who love Me and keep My commandments" (Ex. 20:6, NASB; cf. Deut. 7:9). God showed his lovingkindness to Moses on Mount Sinai when he passed in front of him and said, "The LORD, the LORD God, compassionate and gracious, slow to anger, and abounding in lovingkindness and truth; who keeps lovingkindness for thousands, who forgives iniquity, transgression and sin" (Ex. 34:6-7, NASB).

The lovingkindness of God—that is something worth boasting about. Psalm 136 is one long boast about God's kindness. Twenty-six times God's people utter this refrain: "His lovingkindness is everlasting" (NASB).

To boast about lovingkindness includes boasting in the lavish gift of God's Son, Jesus Christ. "God so loved the world that he gave his one and only Son, that whoever believes in him shall not perish but have eternal life" (John 3:16). It is also to boast about the obedience of Christ when he suffered and died for our sins on the cross. "This is how we know what love is: Jesus Christ laid down his life for us" (1 John 3:16).

Boast about this, too, that the Lord exercises justice on earth. An unjust God is no more to be worshiped than an unkind God. Who would worship a God who lets righteousness go unrewarded or allows wickedness to go unpunished?

The God of the Christian's boast is no such God. He is a God of justice. He condemns the wicked and punishes them with eternal judgment. He vindicates the righteous and rewards them with pleasures forevermore. He will bring every deed to judgment, whether open or secret. God is slow to anger, it is true, but he will not leave the guilty unpunished. He is known for his justice (Ps. 9:16); he loves justice (Ps. 11:7); he gives justice to all the oppressed (Ps. 103:6). A God of such perfect and exacting justice is not to be trifled with. But he is worth boasting about!

Finally, boast about this, that the Lord exercises righteousness on earth. "Righteousness" is uprightness, rectitude, and integrity. It is moral perfection. To say that God is righteous is to say that he is holy, holy, holy (cf. Isa. 6:3). He is upright in all his ways and perfect in all his actions.

To boast about the righteousness of God is really to boast about the righteousness of Jesus Christ. For in the righteousness of Christ, God's lovingkindness and justice embrace. As Jeremiah has already boasted, God is love and God is just. Because of his justice God cannot simply overlook sin: Although that might be loving, it would not be just. Because of his love God did not simply damn us for our sins: Although that would be just, it would not be a full expression of God's love. But love and justice embrace in the righteousness of Christ.

Jesus Christ gave himself up for us all—that is God's lovingkindness. Jesus Christ satisfied the justice of God by paying the price for our sins—that is God's justice. The righteousness of Christ makes God to be both just and the justifier of the ungodly (Rom. 3:26). That is so far beyond anything mortals could improvise that it calls for a boast.

Paul proposes such a boast at the end of his exposition of Jeremiah 9. He moves from worldly wisdom (which is nothing to boast about) to the righteousness of Christ (which is something to boast about):

God chose the foolish things of the world to shame the wise;
God chose the weak things of the world to shame the strong.
He chose the lowly things of this world and the despised
things—and the things that are not—to nullify the things that
are, so that no one may boast before him. It is because of him
that you are in Christ Jesus, who has become for us wisdom
from God—that is, our righteousness, holiness and redemption.
Therefore, as it is written: "Let him who boasts boast in the
Lord." (1 Cor. 1:27-31)

Yes, let everyone who boasts boast in the Lord who exercises
kindness, justice, and righteousness on earth.

Do you know this boastable Lord? If not, then you have
nothing to boast about. If so, then boast all you want. You have
so many reasons to boast you will be boasting away for all
eternity.

CHAPTER 6

THE SCARECROW IN
THE MELON PATCH

Like a scarecrow in a melon patch,
their idols cannot speak;
they must be carried
because they cannot walk.
Do not fear them;
they can do no harm
nor can they do any good. . . .
He who is the Portion of Jacob is not like these,
for he is the Maker of all things,
including Israel, the tribe of his inheritance—
the LORD Almighty is his name.

JEREMIAH 10:5, 16

Jeremiah 10 is a duet in which the prophet weaves two voices together into one song. First one voice sings, then the other, and then the first sings again.

Derek Kidner describes the duet as a polemic and a psalm.[1] A *polemic* is an attack, objection, argument, critique or refutation of something false. The polemical voice in this song speaks out against the idols of the nations and attacks them because they are worthless. A *psalm* is a song of praise. In his psalm Jeremiah praises the matchless God of the universe.

ONLY SKIN DEEP

Jeremiah's duet begins with dark, ominous words, like chords from an organ at the beginning of a suspense film. They give a foreboding sense of impending doom. God promises to punish all the nations of the world who do not worship him: "'The days are coming,' declares the LORD, 'when I will punish all who are circumcised only in the flesh—Egypt, Judah, Edom, Ammon, Moab and all who live in the desert in distant places'" (9:25-26). This is a preview of coming destructions: God is coming soon to a nation near you! The prophecy serves as a precursor of the end of Jeremiah's book, which contains six chapters of judgment against these very nations (chapters 46–51).

Divine judgment comes as no surprise because "these nations are really uncircumcised" (9:26). They do not belong to God, nor do they bear in their bodies the sign of belonging to him.

What is shocking is that God judges Israel along with these unholy nations. He tosses the sacred in with the profane, the circumcised in with the uncircumcised, the clean laundry in with the dirty clothes: "Even the whole house of Israel is uncircumcised in heart" (9:26; cf. Deut. 10:16-17; Jer. 4:4). The people of God have become little more than pagans.

The problem is that Israel's religion is merely external. They are just going through the motions. They practice all the outward traditions of the Law of Moses, but they do not love God with an undying love. They circumcise their bodies but not their hearts, so their faith is only skin deep.

This reminds the Christian of the necessity of living a baptized life. The *Westminster Larger Catechism* calls this "improving our baptism" (Q & A 167). New Testament baptism—like Old Testament circumcision—marks the Christian's entrance into the family of God. It is a sign and a seal of the grace of God. But the act of water baptism does not save. The believer must be baptized in the heart as well as in the flesh, with the Holy Spirit as well as with water (cf. Acts 11:16). Anyone who has been baptized with water but does not live like a Christian is still a pagan.

WHY IDOLS ATTRACT

The reason Jeremiah lumps the Jews in with the other nations is because they have been acting like pagans. The point of his polemic is that his people have been worshiping idols.

Contemporary Christians face a problem when they encounter Old Testament idols. Most have seen enough pictures of ancient Near Eastern artifacts to know that idols are little wooden statues or clay figurines standing on a shelf. They do not impress. They seem more like cultural relics than deities. They are not the kind of things postmodern pagans are tempted to worship.

Understanding how idols work, however, requires sensing their attraction. Calvin explained this in his *Institutes of the Christian Religion*:

> Let us learn how greatly our nature inclines toward idolatry, rather than, by charging the Jews with being guilty of the common failing, we, under vain enticements to sin, sleep the sleep of death.[2]

To put it another way, take the two-by-four out of your own eye before taking the sawdust out of Israel's eye (cf. Luke 6:41-42).

Why is idol worship so attractive to Israel in Jeremiah's day? First, because "everybody's doing it." Idolatry is supported by the weight of public opinion. Jeremiah describes idol worship as one of "the ways of the nations" (Jer. 10:2) and "the customs of the peoples" (10:3). Israel is under international peer pressure. The Babylonians are so successful that everything they do seems glamorous, even their religion. When the Babylonians read the "signs in the sky" (10:2), the Israelites want to check their horoscopes too. If idolatry is good enough for Babylon, it's good enough for Jerusalem.

Israel is fascinated with foreign religion: "Hammered silver is brought from Tarshish and gold from Uphaz" (10:9). Idol worship is "in." It is trendy and fashionable. There are articles about it in the magazines at the grocery store. Idol worship is also exotic. It has all the sophistication of faraway lands. Peer pressure does not end with puberty. The social pressures to worship the wrong things can squeeze entire nations of adults. They might even squeeze you.

The other reason idols attract is aesthetic. Idolatry is beautiful. Ancient idols were adorned with precious metals and overlaid with silver and gold. Then they were richly clothed, like so many mannequins in a department store. They were "dressed in blue and purple," the colors of royalty. The craftsmanship was excellent, "all made by skilled workers" (10:9).

Before laughing at the Israelites for bowing down before blocks of wood, feel the tug of idolatry in your own heart. Consider how attractive the idols of this age often seem. Consider the appeal of rich desserts. Or the satisfaction of managing the lives of others. Or the allure of sexual pleasure. Or the comfort of being well-liked. Or the exhilaration of making it to the top of your profession. Or the relaxation of a luxury vacation. Or the security of good insurance coverage.

All these things can become idols. Origen (c. 185-254), the great African theologian, said, "What each one honors before all else, what before all things he admires and loves, this for him is God." So food, control, sex, popularity, success, leisure, and financial security can all become like gods. They can occupy the place in life that God alone should occupy.

Theologian David Wells defines idolatry as,

> . . . trusting some substitute for God to serve some uniquely
> divine function. . . . These substitutes need not be super-

natural; money, power, expertise, the location of the planets on the astrological charts, and a belief in Progress are
among the most popular idols of Our Time.[3]

Such idols attract. They seem good. The trouble comes when they
take God's place.

Then add to the natural attraction of idolatry the fact that
"everybody's doing it." It seems like everyone is eating like a glut-
ton, fooling around, people-pleasing, climbing the corporate lad-
der, using people to complete an agenda, living a life of ease, or
basing his net worth on his net worth. Contemporary Christians
face as much pressure to be idolaters as Jeremiah's friends did.
Maybe more, since more idols are available.

IF I ONLY HAD A BRAIN

As attractive and popular as idols are, they are still worthless.
Three times Jeremiah says idols are "worthless." The customs of
the people (10:3), wooden idols (10:8), and images (10:15) are
all said to be "worthless." As we have seen, this is Solomon's
word for "vanity." Idols are absolute nothings, total zeroes.

Why are idols so completely worthless? This is the argument
that forms Jeremiah's polemic. First, idols are man-made:

> "For the customs of the peoples are worthless;
>   they cut a tree out of the forest,
>   and a craftsman shapes it with his chisel.
> They adorn it with silver and gold;
>   they fasten it with hammer and nails
>   so it will not totter." (10:3-4)

The prophet gives a do-it-yourself kit for making idols:
Choose a sturdy tree in the forest, chop it down and drag it back
to your workbench. Next, take a hammer and some carving tools

and shape it to look like an animal or a person. Then adorn it with silver and gold.

One more thing: Nail the idol down (10:4). Idols usually go up on the shelf; however, the kind of god who can be shelved runs the risk of toppling over and breaking. There is something embarrassing about a wobbly god, something unseemly about a deity who falls off the shelf and lands on his face. Better to get out the hammer and nail him into place.

Jeremiah is starting to show how ridiculous it is to worship idols. His point is that idols are man-made. They are manufactured in the heart. According to Calvin, human nature "is a perpetual factory of idols."[4]

The problem with man-made idols is that they are impotent, powerless, unable to do anything. They are "like a scarecrow in a melon patch" (10:5).

Jeremiah's analogy suggests that idols are much like the scarecrow in *Wizard of Oz*. As Dorothy followed the Yellow Brick Road on her way to the Emerald City, she passed a scarecrow who was very sad. A tear ran down the poor fellow's cheek.

The reason the Scarecrow was such a sad sack was because he was a few bales short of a haystack. He wistfully tells all the things he would be able to do, think, and say—if he only had a brain: *"My head I'd be scratchin' while my thoughts were busy hatchin' if I only had a brain."*

False gods are like the scarecrow in the melon patch. They do not have any brains (or anything else, for that matter):

> *"Like a scarecrow in a melon patch*
> 	*their idols cannot speak;*
> *they must be carried*
> 	*because they cannot walk.*
> *Do not fear them;*
> 	*they can do no harm*
> 	*nor can they do any good."* (10:5)

False gods cannot speak, think, walk, do any harm or do any good. They cannot save from sin and death. They cannot do anything at all. The most that can be said for idols is that they are portable:

> Jeremiah pictures a tame god, a user-friendly god, who exists by human manufacture, is at human disposal, and is under human control. This god would never rebuke, warn, threaten, or talk back.[5]

Idols appear lifelike, but they are actually lifeless:

> *Everyone is senseless and without knowledge;*
> *every goldsmith is shamed by his idols.*
> *His images are a fraud;*
> *they have no breath in them.* (10:14)

Idolaters are as false as their idols. Even the wise men of the nations "are all senseless and foolish; they are taught by worthless wooden idols" (10:8).

This is Jeremiah's polemic against idolatry: Idols are manmade, impotent, false, and generally worthless. His tone is scornful and sarcastic, which is typical of the way Old Testament prophets treat idols. Elijah is just as scornful in 1 Kings 18 when he taunts the prophets of Baal. Isaiah is equally sarcastic in Isaiah 44 when he ridicules gods made of wood. Idols "are worthless, the objects of mockery" (Jer. 10:15).

The idols in your own heart deserve similar treatment. The first step is to identify them. Dick Keyes points out that most Christians have dozens of idols:

> In this society, our idols tend to be in clusters. They are inflationary, have short shelf lives, and change, adapt, and multiply quickly as if by mitosis, or cell-division. An idol can be a physical property, a person, an activity, a role, an institu-

tion, a hope, an image, an idea, a pleasure, a hero—anything that can substitute for God.[6]

This leaves plenty of scope for idolatry. A piece of merchandise in a mail-order catalog. A potential mate. Collecting antiques. Rollerblading. Popular music. Your ministry in the church. All these things can become idols.

To identify your own idols, ask questions like these: What things take the place of God in my life? Where do I find my significance and my confidence? What things make me really angry? Anger usually erupts when an idol gets knocked off the shelf.

Once the idols on your shelf have been identified, see them for what they really are. Recognize that they are like the scarecrow in the melon patch: man-made, impotent, false, and worthless. Then scorn them the way Jeremiah scorned the idols of his day.

What would a prophet say about our private idolatries? He might say, "Do you mean to tell me that you worship television? You must be joking! The images on your TV screen are not even real. The characters in the soap opera do not deserve your pity; the characters in the sit-com do not deserve your laughter. When you pull the plug, they all vanish."

Or a prophet might say: "You worship your work? You must be out of your mind! Your career cannot give you lasting satisfaction. No one ever says—at a retirement dinner or from a deathbed—'I wish I had spent more time at the office.'"

Or maybe he would say, "You have got to be kidding! You worship . . ." There are not enough pages in this book to list every example. But the Holy Spirit can help identify your idols and figure out what kind of derision they deserve.

GOD, THE ONE AND ONLY

The polemical part of Jeremiah's duet comes wrapped in a psalm that is exceedingly rich in its praise of God's attributes.

Everything Jeremiah praises about God's character stands in direct contrast to everything he criticizes about pagan idols. Where the polemic jangles against the worthlessness of every idol, the psalm sweetly praises the matchlessness of the only God.

Together, the polemic and the psalm comprise an effective strategy for apologetics. Apologetics is a fancy term for explaining why you are a Christian. Biblical apologetics often employs a one-two punch: first a polemic and then a psalm. First an attack on false gods and then a defense of the true God.

This was Elijah's strategy on Mount Carmel: the refutation of Baal before the demonstration of the Lord God of Israel (1 Kings 18). It is also Jeremiah's strategy in his duet. Having proven the worthlessness of idols, he proceeds to show the matchlessness of God. This basic strategy is useful whenever you explain why you are Christian. Start by revealing the weakness of a pagan worldview and end by boasting about salvation in Jesus Christ.

Jeremiah begins his boast with the uniqueness of God. God is one-of-a-kind, incomparable. "No one is like you, O LORD" (Jer. 10:6). Idols are a dime a dozen. There are as many idols as there are scarecrows in all the melon patches in the world. But there is only one God.

Jeremiah presents God, the one-and-only, as a great God. "You are great," he boasts (10:6). Idols are worthless, vain, empty. They cannot even stand on their own two feet without wobbling. But God is great. Even his name is great; it is "mighty in power" (10:6).

Furthermore, God is the "King of the nations" (10:7). An idol can only be in one place at a time. Once the scarecrow gets put in the melon patch, it stays there until it gets moved. But God is everywhere. There is no limit to the extent of the kingdom of Jesus Christ. He deserves reverence from all peoples and nations.

Then add wisdom to God's greatness and sovereign rule. All the wise men in all the nations would not begin to approach the wisdom of God. This is because God is True, with a capital T.

"The LORD is the true God" (10:10). The idols are false, witless, a total sham. Behind their fancy costumes and shiny jewels are nothing but blocks of wood. But God is the genuine article. He is true to his character, true in all he says and does. The one God is the true God.

Moreover, he is "the living God" (10:10). The trouble with scarecrows is that they are not alive. Their heads are full of stuffin'. "They have no breath in them" (10:14). But the one, great, true God is the living God.

It is vastly preferable to have a God who is *alive*. Consider what an advantage it is that Jesus Christ has been raised from the dead. When you pray to him he can answer. When you are sick he can heal you. When you are in trouble he can save you. When you sin he can forgive you. And when you are dead he can bring you back to life.

Jeremiah's psalm praises God as "the eternal King" (10:10). Idols have short shelf-lives. "When their judgment comes, they will perish" (10:15). But the kingdom of God is no temporary monarchy. God is never in danger of being voted out of office. Jesus Christ will be King over heaven and earth forever and forever. "Of the increase of his government and peace there will be no end. He will reign on David's throne and over his kingdom . . . forever" (Isa. 9:7).

Then consider the justice of God's wrath: "When he is angry, the earth trembles; the nations cannot endure his wrath" (Jer. 10:10b). Idols do not make people tremble. At best, scarecrows only frighten blackbirds. But the anger of God against sin will make all nations tremble. Who can withstand his wrath?

Perhaps the most important difference between scarecrows and the living is that scarecrows are manufactured. Idols are man-made. They did not make themselves and cannot make anything else. "These gods, who did not make the heavens and the earth, will perish from the earth and from under the heavens" (10:11).

God is not man-made. On the contrary, God made mankind.

God—the one and only, the true and living Lord, the eternal King—made mankind. He gave life to all that is:

> God made the earth by his power;
>> he founded the world by his wisdom
>> and stretched out the heavens by his understanding. (10:12)

This is God's work of creation, his making the world and everything in it, and all very good. That is what God *did*.

Add what God *does* to what he did. His providence is as much his work as creation is. God did not just wind up the world and then let it wind down, like some cosmic watchmaker. He not only created the world but continues to sustain it by the word of his power:

> When he thunders, the waters in the heavens roar;
>> he makes clouds rise from the ends of the earth.
>> He sends lightning with the rain
>> and brings out the wind
>> from his storehouses. (10:13)

The providence of God extends to the rain, the clouds, the lightning, and the wind.

This is a beautiful psalm written to praise a beautiful God. In it Jeremiah gives an outline for an entire Sunday school class on the doctrine of God. It covers the uniqueness, power, sovereignty, wisdom, truth, eternity, creativity, and providence of God.

A HEALTHY PORTION

It might be tempting to think that an almighty God is out of reach. But Jeremiah has saved the best for last. He dismisses any doubts about our ability to have a friendship with an omnipotent and eternal God with this beautiful title: "He who is the Portion of Jacob is not like these" (10:16).

True, God "is the Maker of all things." But he also made
Israel, "the tribe of his inheritance" (10:16). In addition to making the heavens and the earth, God made a people for himself.
"The LORD's portion is his people" (Deut. 32:9). A "portion" is
a share or allotment of an inheritance. When the children of Israel
entered the Promised Land, they each received a portion of the
land (Josh. 13—19). To say that God's people are his portion is
to say that they belong to him. His people are his by right.
Jeremiah even calls them God's inheritance, as if they were God's
prized possession (which they are!).

At the same time, God belongs to his people. He has entered
into a mutual friendship with them through Jesus Christ. Jesus is
our allotment or inheritance. In Christ, we help ourselves to a
portion of divinity. It is almost as if we can grab a piece of God.
He is our possession. We are entitled to him. He is ours by grace.

To have a healthy portion of God is to have the ultimate
inheritance. If God is your portion, you will not need any sec-
onds. Jeremiah knew this from his own experience. The weeping
prophet was often in deep distress. He wrote about being
afflicted, having his heart pierced, becoming a laughingstock,
having his teeth broken and being downcast (Lam. 3:1-20). But
in the midst of his distress Jeremiah remembered that he had the
ultimate inheritance: "I say to myself, 'The LORD is my portion;
therefore I will wait for him'" (Lam. 3:24; cf. Ps. 73:26; 119:57).
Jeremiah never let go of his portion of God.

It is hard to find such intimacy in the melon patch.
Scarecrows are not much comfort. Consider the scarecrow in Mr.
McGregor's garden. In Beatrix Potter's *Peter Rabbit*, Peter gets
into all kinds of trouble. After he runs into Mr. McGregor
"round the end of a cucumber frame," the old farmer chases him
all over the garden. Along the way Peter loses his entire
wardrobe. He loses one shoe among the cabbages and another
among the potatoes. He gets caught in a gooseberry net by his
buttons and has to wriggle out of his new jacket to get free.

Later, when Peter ventures back into the garden, he discovers that the enterprising Mr. McGregor has appropriated his clothes and turned them into a scarecrow. That is how a scarecrow is made: Nail a few pieces of wood together, throw on a jacket and a pair of shoes and—*voilà*—a scarecrow. This is why it is impossible to develop a relationship with an idol. Sane people do not often carry on conversations with their wardrobes.

Jesus Christ is no scarecrow. He came to this world so his people could enter into friendship with God. Jesus says,

> *"You are my friends if you do what I command. I no longer call you servants, because a servant does not know his master's business. Instead, I have called you friends, for everything that I learned from my Father I have made known to you."* (John 15:14-15)

What a friend we have in Jesus! He is the Christian's allotment and inheritance. The Lord Almighty, who made heaven and earth, is our portion forever.

CHAPTER 7

IN THE

POTTER'S HANDS

"O house of Israel, can I not do with you as this potter does?"
declares the LORD. "Like clay in the hand of the potter, so are
you in my hand, O house of Israel."

JEREMIAH 18:6

It is time for Jeremiah to take another field trip. God has already taken him up and down the streets of Jerusalem (5:1) and around the ruins of Shiloh (7:12). Now he takes him to a pottery workshop. This is the word that came to Jeremiah from the LORD:

> *"Go down to the potter's house, and there I will give you my*
> *message." So I went down to the potter's house, and I saw him*
> *working at the wheel. But the pot he was shaping from the clay*
> *was marred in his hands; so the potter formed it into another*
> *pot, shaping it as seemed best to him." (18:2-4)*

What Jeremiah sees happens all the time in a pottery shop. First, the potter slaps a lump of clay in the middle of his stone wheel. Spinning the wheel with his feet, he deftly begins to shape the clay with his hands, forming it into a pot. But then something goes wrong. The pot is not shaping up properly. There is a flaw in the clay, or perhaps it is inferior for delicate work. So the potter skillfully forms it into a different vessel altogether. He turns a pitcher into a bowl or a lamp into a cup, whatever seems best to him.

The potter's wheel is a lesson in the absolute sovereignty of God. It puts an end to pride and silences every boast. "Then the word of the LORD came to me: 'O house of Israel, can I not do with you as this potter does?'" (18:5-6a). God's question needs no answer. It is one of the great rhetorical questions of the Bible. "Can I not do with you as this potter does?" Who would dare to answer such a question in the negative? "Like clay in the hand of the potter, so are you in my hand, O house of Israel" (18:6b).

HE IS THE POTTER, WE ARE THE CLAY

The doctrine of this passage can be stated very simply: God can do whatever he wants with you. That is what it means for him to be God. Because God is God, he is free to do whatever he pleases. In his hands rest all power, rule, control, authority, kingdom, government, and dominion.

This is the doctrine of the sovereignty of God. Some people do not care for this doctrine. Others tremble at it. Some may even try to oppose it. But it cannot be denied. Human beings are not on equal terms with God. He is the Creator; we are the creatures. God is the absolute sovereign; all others are total subservients. "Does the clay say to the potter, 'What are you making?'" (Isa. 45:9).

The picture of potter and clay is doubly appropriate to describe God's relationship to us. First, we are made of clay. The *Catechism for Young Children* asks, "Of what were our first parents made?" (Q 17). The answer begins like this: "God made the body of Adam out of the ground" (A 17). This is taken right from Scripture: "The LORD God formed the man from the dust of the ground" (Gen. 2:7). God was the Potter, Adam was the clay. The Hebrew word Jeremiah uses for "potter" (*yotzer*) comes from the word "formed" (*yatzar*) in Genesis 2. The first thing we learn about our position in the universe with respect to God is that he is the Potter and we are the clay.

If this was true at Creation, it is all the more true after the Fall. When Adam sinned, God cursed humanity:

> *"By the sweat of your brow*
> *you will eat your food*
> *until you return to the ground,*
> *since from it you were taken;*
> *for dust you are*
> *and to dust you will return."* (Gen. 3:19)

God turned the dust into clay to form a pot. After a little while, the pot will return to dust. "Ashes to ashes, dust to dust."

Since the beginning of the world, human beings have known that they are dust. King David wrote, "You lay me in the dust of death" (Ps. 22:15). When Hamlet knelt beside a grave to hold poor Yorick's skull, he imagined the great emperors of the world reduced to dust, with their dirt then put to some common use:

> *Alexander died, Alexander was buried, Alexander returneth*
> *into dust; the dust is earth; of earth we make loam; and why of*
> *that loam, whereto he was converted, might they not stop a*
> *beer-barrel?*
>> *Imperious Caesar, dead and turn'd to clay,*
>> *Might stop a hole to keep the wind away:*
>> *O, that that earth, which kept the world in awe,*
>> *Should patch a wall to expel the winter's flaw!*[1]

The dustiness of humanity is recognized to the present day. "Dust in the wind," sang the popular singing group Kansas. "All we are is dust in the wind." On *Star Trek: The Next Generation* human beings are referred to as "carbon units." It may sound insulting, but it is sound theology, not to mention good science.

The bodies of human beings are made from the dust of the ground. We are but clay.

The picture of the potter and the clay is also appropriate because a potter can do whatever he wants with clay. Wet clay is malleable. A skilled craftsperson can shape it into almost anything. Just the slightest adjustment of the thumb or fingers changes the contours of a pot. The potter has complete mastery over the clay.

Have you ever seen a potter's arms? I once saw a potter challenge anyone in a large congregation to an arm wrestling match. Although she was a small woman she did not get any takers. Not after she flexed her massive forearms anyway! Her muscles were strong from years of shaping pots. In the strong hands of a potter, clay will be pounded and shaped however the potter pleases.

If we are clay, then we are at the Potter's mercy. Calvin wrote,

> Until then men are brought to know that they are so subject to God's power that their condition can in a single moment be changed, according to his will, they will never be humble as they ought to be.[2]

God can do whatever he wants with us.

CLAY IN THE HANDS OF AN ANGRY POTTER

Though familiar, Jeremiah's image of the potter and the clay is often misunderstood. Some scholars say the potter is limited by his clay:

> The quality of the clay determined what the potter could do with it. He could make something else from the same clay, but not the particular vessel he had hoped for. The clay could thus frustrate the potter's original intention and cause him to change it. Yahweh the potter was dealing with

a clay that was resistant to his purpose. The quality of the people in some way determined what God might do with them.[3]

This viewpoint gives too much credit to the clay and too little to the Potter. It forgets that this Potter *made* his clay in the first place. It allows the clay to control its own destiny, as if mere human beings could change the mind of God.

The prophet Isaiah had a good answer for scholars who exalt humanity at the expense of deity:

> *You turn things upside down,*
> *   as if the potter were thought to be like the clay!*
> *Shall what is formed say to him who formed it,*
> *   "He did not make me"?*
> *Can the pot say of the potter,*
> *   "He knows nothing"?* (Isa. 29:16)

If God is the Potter, then let him be the Potter!

Others assume that the picture of God as Potter is comforting. They take these verses to mean something like this: "God isn't finished with me yet. He is making me into something beautiful." As we shall see, there is some truth in this idea. But it is not Jeremiah's main point.

Jeremiah's message is about judgment. The picture of the pot on the potter's wheel is not meant to be comforting. Like much modern art, it is meant to be disturbing. Jeremiah's message is about clay in the hands of an angry Potter. If God can do whatever he wants, then he has the right to destroy you for your sins. God is the one who brought you into this world, and he can take you out of it. Until you recognize this, you have not fully reckoned with the sovereignty of God.

The reason God took Jeremiah down to the potter's house was to warn Israel about the wrath of God. He begins with the ultimate reason for the rise and fall of nations:

"If at any time I announce that a nation or kingdom is to be uprooted, torn down and destroyed, and if that nation I warned repents of its evil, then I will relent and not inflict on it the disaster I had planned. And if at another time I announce that a nation or kingdom is to be built up and planted, and if it does evil in my sight and does not obey me, then I will reconsider the good I have intended to do for it." (Jer. 18:7-10)

These are general principles for the way God deals with the kingdoms of this world. God does not just make a wine jar here and a flowerpot there. Entire nations are shaped upon his wheel. He brings prosperity or disaster as he pleases. His prophet Jeremiah was appointed "over nations and kingdoms to uproot and tear down, to destroy and overthrow, to build and to plant" (1:10). A kingdom heading for destruction will be saved if it repents of its sins. On the other hand, a nation once blessed by God will be destroyed for its wickedness.

These are words of warning for America at the dawn of the new millennium. The United States is an empire in decline, seemingly headed for destruction. When will it be "uprooted, torn down and destroyed"? Harold O. J. Brown has observed that "it would take someone with a supernatural gift of prophecy to tell us the number of days or weeks or years that the American commonwealth can be expected to endure without . . . being overthrown. . . . But it does not take a prophetic gift to see that . . . disaster on a national scale is inevitable."

According to Jeremiah, the only way to escape such disaster is to turn away from sin. The only way to get God to relent is for Americans to repent for their hatred and violence, wastefulness and sloth, racism and injustice, selfishness, materialism, and sexual immorality. According to the Word of God a sinful nation must either repent or perish.

What is especially sad about America's spiritual condition is that it was once a nation "built up and planted" by God (18:9).

Christians often exaggerate the extent to which ours has been a Christian nation, but there is no doubt that God has shed his grace on America. The first colonists came to the New World to establish a Christian community living in covenant with God. The Constitution of the United States is based largely on biblical principles. God rewarded that solid foundation by making America a blessing to the world, using the nation to bring tyrants to justice and to pioneer in the work of worldwide missions. But the United States is mere clay, and God is the Potter. He will mold or mar as he pleases, according to the righteousness and repentance of the nation.

God gave the same message to Jerusalem in the days of Jeremiah. After setting forth his general principles for ruling the nations, he applied them to his own people:

> "Look! I am preparing a disaster for you and devising a plan against you. So turn from your evil ways, each one of you, and reform your ways and your actions." (18:11)

The people of God are clay in the hands of an angry Potter.

LET'S GET JEREMIAH!

Given the choice between repenting or perishing, one might think Israel would repent. Sadly, this clay rejects God's message. "It's no use," they reply. "We will continue with our own plans; each of us will follow the stubbornness of his evil heart" (18:12). Like most toddlers, the children of Israel have their own agenda. Now that they have made their plans, there is no hope of getting them to submit to God's will.

The reason God's people are so stubborn is that they have forgotten God. They have a case of national amnesia. No one has ever heard anything like it (18:13); it is like a freak of nature. "Does the snow of Lebanon ever vanish from its rocky slopes?" (18:14a).

Not at that altitude. "Do its cool waters from distant sources ever cease to flow?" (18:14b). No, they are fed by living springs.

> *"Yet my people have forgotten me;*
> *   they burn incense to worthless idols,*
> *which made them stumble in their ways*
> *and in the ancient paths.*
> *They made them walk in bypaths*
> *   and on roads not built up." (18:15)*

Jeremiah is returning to one of his favorite themes. Already he has compared Israel to a bride who forgets her wedding ornaments (2:32). That would be unthinkable, yet God's people have forgotten their love for God. Already Jeremiah has stood at the crossroads and mapped out the best path for his people (6:16; cf. 12:5). But now they are taking a shortcut, leaving God's highway to careen out of control down the back roads of idolatry. Jeremiah is shocked by their behavior. He senses that "a most horrible thing has been done by Virgin Israel" (18:13).

These verses contain a strong warning for anyone who was raised in the church but has wandered away from God. Once you claimed to be a Christian. Once you read your Bible and prayed. Once you acted like a follower of Jesus Christ. But now you have spiritual amnesia. You did not mean to end up so far away from God, but look where you are! It is time to wake up before it is too late.

It has turned out to be too late for Jerusalem. Amnesia soon turns into enmity:

> *They said, "Come, let's make plans against Jeremiah; for the teaching of the law by the priest will not be lost, nor will counsel from the wise, nor the word from the prophets. So come, let's attack him with our tongues and pay no attention to anything he says." (18:18)*

Those who begin to forget God end up hating him.

First the Israelites rejected God's message; now they attack his messenger. The leaders hatch another conspiracy. They try to shut Jeremiah up. "Other priests can teach the law," they say. "Other wise men can give good counsel. Other prophets can speak the Word of the Lord. But we have no use for Jeremiah." Though the prophet has done them good, they will repay him with evil. Though Jeremiah often has prayed for them, they have dug a pit to capture him (18:20).

What happens to people who reject God's message and attack his messenger? They are just clay, remember, so God has the right to do whatever he wants with them:

> *"Their land will be laid waste,*
> *an object of lasting scorn;*
> *all who pass by will be appalled*
> *and will shake their heads.*
> *Like a wind from the east,*
> *I will scatter them before their enemies;*
> *I will show them my back and not my face*
> *in the day of their disaster." (18:16-17)*

Ashes to ashes, dust to dust. God will blow them away and then turn his back on them.

They will receive the terrible judgments for which Jeremiah prays. Their children will go hungry; their wives will become widows; their men will be put to death; their young men will be slain in battle (18:21). All these things happened when the Babylonians attacked Israel. A cry went up from the houses in Jerusalem as invaders suddenly attacked (18:22).

Was it right for Jeremiah to pray like this? Was it charitable to ask God not to "forgive their crimes or blot out their sins" (18:23)? Jeremiah seems to go beyond seeking vindication to being vindictive. At least he does not display the mercy of the Lord Jesus Christ, who prayed for his enemies and forgave his executioners.

Jeremiah may have been in the wrong, but God himself has the right to do all the things the prophet prays for. He has the right to repay evil with evil. He has the right to put his enemies to the sword. He has the right to let them fall into their own traps. He is not obligated to forgive those who plot against him. After all, he is the Potter.

Jeremiah 18 should strike holy fear into the heart of every mortal. You are only a lump of clay, spinning and spinning on the Potter's wheel. The God who made you can destroy you without a moment's notice. Any potter will smash a pot in an instant if it bears the slightest defect.

Are there any defects in your life? Any sinful attitudes? Any evil deeds? God has just cause to collapse you upon the wheel. Yet before he turns his back forever—"the time of your anger," Jeremiah calls it (18:23)—he gives you an opportunity to turn back to him.

Ask the Potter for mercy. Beg God to forgive your sins. Trust in Jesus Christ for salvation, believing he died on the cross for you.

> As a father has compassion on his children,
>> so the LORD has compassion on those who fear him;
> for he knows how we are formed,
>> he remembers that we are dust. (Ps. 103:13-14)

God knows you are formed from dust, and sinful dust at that. He has compassion on all who fear him.

A WORK IN PROGRESS

The main reason God took Jeremiah down to the potter's house was to warn about judgment. But the picture of the potter and the clay also gives comfort. If God is the Potter, then he can make something out of the most unpromising blobs of clay. This also is part of his sovereignty.

As Eugene Peterson points out,

No one has ever been able to make a clay pot that is *just* a clay pot. Every pot is also an art form. Pottery is always changing its shape as potters find new proportions, different ways to shape the pots in pleasing combinations of curves. There is no pottery that besides being useful does not also show evidence of beauty. Pottery is artistically shaped, designed, painted, glazed, fired. It is one of the most functional items in life; it is also one of the most beautiful. . . . Useful and beautiful. Functionally necessary and artistically elegant at one and the same time with no thought that the two elements could be separated.[4]

It takes a patient artist to make a pot that is beautiful as well as useful. It takes the kind of potter Jeremiah watched, one who refuses to give up on his work. When there was a flaw in the clay, he did not throw it away; he worked it into something else. F. B. Meyer calls that pot "a memorial of the potter's patience and long-suffering, of his careful use of material, and of his power of repairing loss and making something out of failure and disappointment."[5]

The same could be said of God's people Israel. Though they would be crushed for a time, as Jeremiah prophesied, God remade them into a beautiful kingdom.

The same could also be said of every Christian. We come into this world like so many clay pots. Our lives are pitted with blemishes and impurities. We are neither useful nor beautiful. As clay goes, we are not easy to work with. We need to be created all over again, which is what the Holy Spirit does in the life of a sinner who trusts in Christ. He makes him or her into something useful and beautiful. If you know Christ, then you are a memorial to God's patience and long-suffering, his careful use of material, and his power of making something out of failure.

Are you happy with the way God is shaping your life? God

often makes something out of us that we do not have in mind. We have disappointments in love. We have diseases in our bodies. We have discouragements in our work. We have desperations in our families. For one reason or another, we are often unhappy with the way life is shaping up. Very likely, if you were behind the potter's wheel, you would make you differently. Would you then try to fashion yourself into the Potter and unseat God from the wheel?

You are not the Potter. You are only clay. The proper thing for clay to do is trust the Potter and yield to his hands. Ulrich Zwingli once wrote to a friend, "I beseech Christ for this one thing only, that he will enable me to endure all things courageously, and that he break me as a potter's vessel or make me strong, as it pleases him."[6]

Are you willing to trust the Potter? Do you believe that he knows best, designs best, shapes best, fashions best? If you have given your heart to God, you can trust him to transform you into something useful and beautiful. If that seems hard to believe, it is because he is not even close to being finished yet. He is taking the time to work on the parts of your life that are still lumpy and off-center. Some parts he may need to smash down and raise up all over again. Will you trust him—really trust him—to do what is best?

Adelaide Pollard (1862-1934) has written a prayer for willing clay, the kind of clay that stays on the wheel to be shaped in the Potter's hands:

> *Have thine own way, Lord! Have thine own way!*
> *Thou art the potter; I am the clay.*
> *Mold me and make me after thy will,*
> *While I am waiting, yielded and still.*
> *Have thine own way, Lord! Have thine own way!*
> *Hold o'er my being absolute sway!*
> *Fill with thy Spirit till all shall see*
> *Christ only, always, living in me!*

CHAPTER 8

DARK NIGHT

OF THE SOUL

Whenever I speak, I cry out
proclaiming violence and destruction.
So the word of the LORD has brought me
   insult and reproach all day long.
But if I say, "I will not mention him
or speak any more in his name,"
his word is in my heart like a fire,
a fire shut up in my bones.
I am weary of holding it in;
   indeed, I cannot.

JEREMIAH 20:8-9

The writer Kathleen Norris once spent a year and a half with the Benedictine monks of St. John's Abbey in Minnesota. During her stay she discovered that an important part of monastic life is the continuous reading of entire books of the Bible, section by section, during morning and evening prayer.

By the end of her sabbatical Norris had heard the entire New Testament and large portions of the Old. She writes,

The most remarkable experience of all was plunging into the prophet Jeremiah at morning prayer in late September one year, and staying with him through mid-November. We began with chapter 1, and read straight through, ending at chapter 22:17. Listening to Jeremiah is . . . a way to get your blood going in the morning; it puts caffeine to shame.[1]

Norris goes on to explain how Jeremiah's sufferings became the agonies of her own soul:

> Opening oneself to a prophet as anguished as Jeremiah is painful. On some mornings, I found it impossible. . . . The voice of Jeremiah is compelling, often on an overwhelmingly personal level. One morning, I was so worn out by the emotional roller coaster of chapter 20 that after prayers I walked to my apartment and went back to bed. This passionate soliloquy, which begins with a bitter outburst on the nature of the prophet's calling, moves quickly into denial. Jeremiah's anger at the way his enemies deride him rears up, and also fear and sorrow. His statement of confidence in God seems forced under the circumstances, and a brief doxology feels more ironic than not, being followed by a bitter cry. The chapter concludes with an anguished question.[2]

Jeremiah 20 gives plenty of reasons to dive back under the covers. It is the low point of Jeremiah's ministry, his dark night of the soul. In it he blames God, rejects his calling, and curses the day he was born.

JEREMIAH DOES TIME

The man to blame for Jeremiah's despair is a priest named Pashhur. As chief of security at the temple, Pashhur is in charge of the prophecy police. He has heard that Jeremiah dashed a clay pot to the ground in the Valley of Ben Hinnom (19:1-15). He has also heard the gist of the prophecy Jeremiah uttered in the precincts of the temple, that Jerusalem was about to be smashed to smithereens (20:1). It sounds like treason, so Pashhur has God's prophet arrested, "beaten and put in the stocks at the

Upper Gate of Benjamin at the LORD's temple" (20:2). Post-Christian regimes are not always congenial to God's disciples.

Jeremiah has been threatened before, but this time the authorities are taking action. First they thrash him and then they torture him. Putting Jeremiah in "stocks" means more than just locking him up. The Hebrew word refers to twisting (*mahpeket*). They put Jeremiah on the rack, clamping his wrists and twisting his body into painful contortions.

What Pashhur did was very wicked. Apparently he feels some remorse, because he frees Jeremiah the next morning. But the damage has already been done. Pashhur has beaten the Lord's anointed. Opposing the Lord's faithful ministers always brings a curse.

Upon his release, Jeremiah greets Pashhur with a message of judgment—not from himself but from the Lord:

> "The LORD's name for you is not Pashhur, but Magor-Missabib. For this is what the LORD says: 'I will make you a terror to yourself and to all your friends; with your own eyes you will see them fall by the sword of their enemies. I will hand all Judah over to the king of Babylon, who will carry them away to Babylon or put them to the sword. I will hand over to their enemies all the wealth of this city—all its products, all its valuables and all the treasures of the kings of Judah. They will take it away as plunder and carry it off to Babylon. And you, Pashhur, and all who live in your house will go into exile to Babylon. There you will die and be buried, you and all your friends to whom you have prophesied lies.'" (20:3-6)

This prophecy is significant for what it says about Judah. Jeremiah has often warned that judgment would come from the north, but until now he has not mentioned the invader by name. Here, for the first time, we learn that Babylon will be the instrument of divine judgment. From this point on, Jeremiah will mention that fierce city more than two hundred times.

The prophecy also has relevance for Pashhur. Jeremiah's back is still throbbing, and his wrists are still chafing from his imprisonment. But Pashhur's punishment will be even more severe. His friends will fall by the sword or die in captivity (20:4, 6), a prophecy that will surely put a damper on his social life. His lies will be exposed, and his crimes will be repaid with death (20:6). Jeremiah even has the satisfaction of giving Pashhur a nickname that is bound to stick: Magor-Missabib. Pashhur means "fruitful on every side," but Magor-Missabib means "terror on every side" (20:3; cf. 20:10).

TAKE IT TO THE LORD IN PRAYER

That is the story, but not the whole story. It does not tell what went through Jeremiah's mind during his night in jail. Jeremiah 20 is best understood as the prophet's account of his night in the stocks, his dark night of the soul.

There are at least four valuable lessons about suffering in these verses. They are relevant for all times because Christians always suffer, but they are especially relevant for pagan times.

The first lesson is perhaps the most important: *Suffering may be taken to the Lord in prayer.* Jeremiah has good reason to be discouraged. For one thing, he is in danger:

> *I hear many whispering,*
> *"Terror on every side!*
> *Report him! Let's report him!"*
> *All my friends*
> *are waiting for me to slip, saying,*
> *"Perhaps he will be deceived;*
> *then we will prevail over him*
> *and take our revenge on him." (20:10)*

The priests are gathering in the corners of the temple. Jeremiah hears their nasty whispers and sees their bony fingers pointed in his direction. Even his friends wait for him to take a false step so they can pounce on him. He has already been beaten and locked up. What will they do to him next? Jeremiah's persecution may only be beginning.

The prophet is also discouraged because he has become a laughingstock: "I am ridiculed all day long; everyone mocks me" (20:7b). The comedians in Jerusalem are getting their funniest material at Jeremiah's expense. "There goes that crazy old Jeremiah. Did you hear what he did yesterday? He took a brand new pot and smashed it outside the city walls. The guy needs a straitjacket. He keeps babbling about enemies coming to destroy the city."

One insult is especially vicious. They call Jeremiah Magor-Missabib, "Terror on every side" (20:10). In other words, they have taken his rebuke of Pashhur and used it against him. Verbal abuse may not seem very serious compared to a good beating, but eventually ridicule starts to take its toll. Jeremiah is despised and rejected.

Jeremiah's friends betray him, even the closest friend of all: "O LORD, you deceived me, and I was deceived; you overpowered me and prevailed" (20:7a). Jeremiah is starting to doubt whether the Word of God is really true after all. God forced him to prophesy, and he prophesied, but where is the promised judgment? Has Jeremiah become a false prophet? He thinks he has been speaking the Word of the Lord, but maybe the Lord has deceived him (cf. 1 Kings 22:22-23; Ezek. 14:9).

The only thing Jeremiah can do with his doubts and sufferings is take them to the Lord in prayer. He offers the prayer of a suffering believer. One can imagine him in solitary confinement, exhausted by physical and emotional pain. The very first words out of his mouth are an invocation: "O LORD," he cries.

God gives us permission to take our sufferings directly to him. This is what the godly have done throughout history. It is what Job did on the ash heap, when he lamented the loss of his

family (Job 3). It is what Elijah did under the broom tree, when
he wanted the Lord to take his life (1 Kings 19:4-5). It is what
David did in the cave, when he fled from Saul (Ps. 57). It is what
Jonah did in the belly of the whale, when he ran away from God
(Jonah 2). It is even what Jesus Christ did on the cross, when he
was crucified to atone for his people's sins: "My God, my God,
why have you forsaken me?" (Matt. 27:46).

Take your sufferings to that secret place where you meet God
in prayer. That is where you must take them. Where else can you
unburden your heart so freely? Who else will comfort you so ten-
derly? There is no need to hide your troubles. Take them to the
Lord in prayer the way Jeremiah did.

FIRE IN THE BONES

The second lesson Jeremiah teaches about suffering is that *believers sometimes suffer for God's sake.* Jeremiah knows why people hate him. The needle seems to be stuck in the same place on
his record album. People are getting sick of hearing him preach
judgment:

> *Whenever I speak, I cry out*
> *proclaiming violence and destruction.*
> *So the word of the Lord has brought me*
> *insult and reproach all day long.* (Jer. 20:8)

God is to blame for Jeremiah's problems. It is not the
prophet's fault he is being insulted all day long. He just says whatever God tells him to say. Although people like Pashhur are blam-
ing the messenger, their real problem is with the message.
Jeremiah is suffering for God's sake.

Jeremiah comes up with a possible solution to his problem. "I
will not mention him or speak any more in his name" (20:9a). He

says, "That's it. I'm through. I'm going to hang up my sandals and get a real job. I will not speak the Word of the Lord any longer." There is only one problem with trying to keep God's Word bottled up inside:

> If I say, "I will not mention him
> or speak any more in his name,"
> his word is in my heart like a fire,
> a fire shut up in my bones.
> I am weary of holding it in;
> indeed, I cannot. (20:9)

This is another familiar text from Jeremiah that is usually taken out of context. It is often used as an inspirational verse for preachers. And so it is. The Word of God *is* like an unquenchable, uncontainable fire in the bones of the gospel minister. I sit at my desk with the Scriptures open before me, longing for the return of the Lord's Day. I labor during the week with a holy impatience for the call to worship to be read, the hymns to be sung, and the offering to be collected so the sermon can begin. There are times when the Word of God weighs upon me so heavily that preaching is a catharsis, the release of a burden seemingly too great to bear a moment longer.

When Jeremiah speaks about the fire in his bones, however, he is not speaking about the pleasures of ministry. He is not testifying to the delights of preaching in the Holy Spirit. He is not saying that his heart is aflame with the Gospel. No, his heart is burning with judgment. The fiery word in his bones is law rather than grace. He is not eager to preach, but reluctant, for he knows that judgment will pour out as soon as he opens his mouth. Jeremiah would give anything to have a mute ministry, but the Word of God will not allow him to be silent. The fire in his bones must blaze forth from his lips.

This reminds those who teach or preach to say only what

God says in his Word. This is one of the great lessons of Jeremiah's ministry. He is surrounded by false prophets who say whatever people want to hear. They say, "Peace, peace," even when there is no peace (6:14; 8:11). But Jeremiah is a true prophet. The distinguishing mark of a true prophet is that he preaches nothing except God's Word. When there is peace Jeremiah says "Peace," but when there is no peace he says "No peace." Faithful ministers preach law as well as grace, justice as well as mercy, judgment as well as salvation. Authentic preaching disturbs as well as comforts.

Sometimes preaching leads to suffering. Proclaiming the true Word of God may lead to opposition, hostility, and even persecution, as it did for Jeremiah. Sometimes believers suffer for the sake of God's Word, especially if they live in a culture that has turned its back on God.

At such times the Christian lives by God's calling. Jeremiah needed to take courage from the promises God made when he first commissioned him to be a prophet:

> "I have made you a fortified city, an iron pillar and a bronze wall to stand against the whole land—against the kings of Judah, its officials, its priests and the people of the land. They will fight against you but will not overcome you, for I am with you and will rescue you," declares the LORD. (1:18-19)

That commission made it clear that Jeremiah would suffer for God's sake. Yet the Lord promised more than suffering; he promised that his prophet would be saved.

Jesus Christ makes the same promise to his disciples. Once he explained how they would suffer for his sake. They would be mistreated and hated by the world. For Christ's sake, they would even be put to death, as events later confirmed. But Jesus ended with a promise: "I have told you these things, so that in me you may have peace. In this world you will have trouble. But take heart! I have overcome the world" (John 16:33).

That is a wonderful verse to commit to memory and apply to daily life. Christians have many troubles in this world. We are sometimes depressed, often disheartened, frequently discouraged. Sometimes we ask, "Why is this happening to me?" Jesus teaches that suffering for God's sake is not a surprise. In this world you will have trouble. But take heart! Christ has overcome the world.

A CALL TO WORSHIP

Jeremiah takes heart during his dark night of the soul. Suddenly, he interrupts his complaint to hold a mini worship service. He is alone and afraid, depressed and discouraged, but he offers a short psalm of praise to God (Jer. 20:11-13). From this a third lesson is to be learned: *God is always to be praised, even in the midst of suffering.*

Jeremiah's worship service is short but complete. His psalm has three elements: a confession of faith, a prayer for deliverance, and a hymn of praise.

Jeremiah's confession of faith reads like this:

> *The LORD is with me like a mighty warrior;*
> *so my persecutors will stumble and not prevail.*
> *They will fail and be thoroughly disgraced;*
> *their dishonor will never be forgotten.* (20:11)

Jeremiah does not understand what is happening to him. Even the Lord seems to be against him. But he testifies to what he knows to be true about God's character:

Here the Prophet sets up God's aid against all the plottings formed against him. However, then, might perfidious friends on one hand try privately to entrap him, and open enemies might on the other hand publicly oppose him, he yet doubted not but that God would be a sufficient protection to him.[3]

Jeremiah knows the Lord is with him even though he *feels* far away. He knows the Lord is strong even though he *seems* powerless. He knows the wicked will be defeated even though they *appear* to triumph. So the prophet boldly confesses that the Lord will save him.

Next, Jeremiah prays for help:

> O LORD Almighty, you who examine the righteous
>   and probe the heart and mind,
> let me see your vengeance upon them,
>   for to you I have committed my cause. (20:12)

Jeremiah does not take matters into his own hands, but commits his cause to the Lord. He prays that he will be vindicated and his enemies will be punished.

Jeremiah closes his worship with a hymn of praise. He bursts into song:

> Sing to the LORD!
>   Give praise to the LORD!
> He rescues the life of the needy
>   from the hands of the wicked. (20:13)

One can imagine Jeremiah bent over in his stocks as he sings. He may not have breath to sing a long hymn, but he can manage at least a short song of praise. Like Paul and Silas after him (Acts 16:25), he praises the Lord in prison.

It is also possible that Jeremiah added this stanza to his song *after* he was released from prison. It is striking that the psalm refers to the needy person in the singular. Literally, the Lord "rescues the life of the needy one" (Jer. 20:13), meaning the prophet himself. He has come through his doubts to a place of strong confidence in the Lord. Jeremiah shows how to praise God during the dark night of the soul.

Like Jeremiah, the German theologian Dietrich Bonhoeffer (1906-1945) was imprisoned for the sake of God's Word. Bonhoeffer endured his dark night of the soul in a Nazi concentration camp. Yet he did not stop praising God:

> I am lonely, but Thou leavest me not.
> I am restless, but with Thee there is peace.[4]

It is always good to praise the Lord, but especially when one is suffering. The best thing to do when you are discouraged is to go to worship. Keep confessing, keep praying, keep singing. Even when you have a complaint to make to God, confess your faith in him, pray for deliverance, and praise his name.

THE FINAL QUESTION

It is tempting to end with Jeremiah's psalm of praise, but that is not how the prophet ends. The Bible must be taken as it comes, and this time it ends on a downer:

> Cursed be the day I was born!
>   May the day my mother bore me not be blessed!
> Cursed be the man who brought my father the news,
>   who made him very glad, saying,
>   "A child is born to you—a son!"
> May that man be like the towns
>   the LORD overthrew without pity.
> May he hear wailing in the morning,
>   a battle cry at noon.
> For he did not kill me in the womb,
>   with my mother as my grave,
>   her womb enlarged forever. (20:14-17)

Instead of celebrating his birthday Jeremiah curses it. He wants to reach back into history and curse everything and everyone who had anything to do with the day of his birth. He wishes the man who brought his father the "good news" had strangled him instead. He wishes God would treat him the way he treated Sodom and Gomorrah.[5]

Jeremiah's mood swings from praising to cursing with dizzying speed. One verse is a paean of high praise; the next is an imprecation of utter despair. Some scholars have concluded that verse 14 "can hardly belong after verse 13."[6] They view chapter 20 as a hodge-podge of Jeremiah's sayings. Even Calvin is mystified; to him it seems "a levity unworthy of the holy man to pass suddenly from thanksgiving to God into imprecations, as though he had forgotten himself."[7]

Perhaps Jeremiah had forgotten himself, but these verses do belong together. They may not belong together by logic, but who says the life of the soul is always logical? Jeremiah's curses follow his praises because that is the way it was during his dark night of the soul.

We must recognize the confusing, almost schizophrenic nature of the Christian life. We are at one and the same time saints and sinners. Although our sins are forgiven, we continue to sin. One minute we praise, and the next we curse; one moment we rejoice in God's plan, and the very next we resist his will.

Jeremiah's curses form a bitter lament, the bitterest in the book of Jeremiah, if not in all of Scripture. Derek Kidner observes that they are intended

> to bowl us over. Together with other tortured cries from him and his fellow sufferers, these raw wounds in Scripture remain lest we forget the sharpness of the age-long struggle, or the frailty of the finest overcomers.[8]

Jeremiah stops just short of cursing God or his parents, which were capital offenses in Israel (Lev. 20:9). He does not actually think about ending it all, but he does wish it had never started:

> *Why did I ever come out of the womb*
> *to see trouble and sorrow*
> *and to end my days in shame?* (Jer. 20:18)

Jeremiah has known the trouble of persecution, the sorrow of watching his people reject God's word, and the shame of public humiliation. All this suffering places a giant question mark over his very existence. Though he is strong in his faith, there are times when he has more questions than answers. Here he questions his creation, his salvation, and his vocation.[9]

Jeremiah's queries teach a final lesson about suffering: *Although suffering can place a question mark over existence, it never has the last word.* Chapter 20 ends with a question Jeremiah himself is in no shape to answer, but Scripture does provide a good answer for it. Why did Jeremiah come out of the womb to see trouble and sorrow?

As we have seen, God has already given Jeremiah the answer—when first he called him into the ministry. The prophet needs to be reminded of the first thing the Lord ever said to him:

> *"Before I formed you in the womb I knew you,*
> *before you were born I set you apart;*
> *I appointed you as a prophet to the nations."* (1:5)

Jeremiah traces his troubles back to the womb. But he is not going back far enough! God traces his promises back before the womb. He had a purpose for Jeremiah's life since before the beginning of time. The prophet needs to be reminded that the Lord has set him apart from all eternity for salvation and ministry.

Perhaps you need the same reminder. Are you suffering? Are

you ridiculed by your friends or family? Are enemies waiting to trip you up? Are you weighed down by the ungodliness of contemporary society? Are there times when you wonder why you ever came out of your mother's womb?

This is why. God set you apart for salvation and for ministry. Before the beginning of time he planned to save you in Christ. "For he chose us in him before the creation of the world" (Eph. 1:4). Then he set you apart to do his work. "For we are God's workmanship, created in Christ Jesus to do good works, which God prepared in advance for us to do" (Eph. 2:10). Suffering can place a giant question mark over our lives, but the grace of God always has the last word.

CHAPTER 9

THE BEST-MADE PLANS

"Seek the peace and prosperity of the city to which I have carried you into exile. Pray to the LORD for it, because if it prospers, you too will prosper. . . . For I know the plans I have for you," declares the LORD, "plans to prosper you and not to harm you, plans to give you hope and a future."

JEREMIAH 29:7, 11

It has finally happened. For decades Jeremiah has prophesied judgment upon God's people. Over and over again he has said God would punish them with sword, famine, and captivity. He has turned out to be right. Jeremiah knows what he has been prophesying about. In the year 597 B.C. the Babylonians swoop down and attack Jerusalem, killing many and carrying most of the rest into captivity.

When judgment finally arrives something remarkable happens. Jeremiah changes his tune. The next several chapters are filled with some of the most wonderful promises in all of Scripture. After twenty-eight chapters of gloom and doom, Jeremiah bears tidings of grace and glory. God will bring his people back from captivity (30:3). He will "love" them "with an everlasting love" (31:3) and "turn their mourning into gladness" (31:13). He will make a "new covenant" (31:31) with them and give them "singleness of heart and action" (32:39). God will even "cleanse them from all the sin they have committed" (33:8).

All these blessings are summarized in one wonderful promise: "'For I know the plans I have for you,'" declares the LORD, "'plans to prosper you and not to harm you, plans to give you hope and a future'" (29:11). God knows what he is doing. He has known it all along, as he always does. God makes his plan and then he carries it out. Everything he does is for the ultimate good of his people.

The promise of Jeremiah 29:11 is precious to me because it is the theme verse for our family. We take an illuminated copy of it wherever we live and mount it on the wall.

I used to think I understood the promise well, but there is something I did not understand about it until we moved to Philadelphia. One evening I stood in the Delancey Lobby of the Tenth Presbyterian Church paging through Robert Linthicum's book, *City of God, City of Satan*. My eye was arrested by his exposition of Jeremiah 29:

> My daughter and her family live near the U.S. city of Detroit. Recently when I was there to visit, I noticed a rather intriguing plaque hanging on the wall of their home. It was a photograph with golden lettering on it. The photograph was any camera buff's dream—pine trees near the foreground framing the picture, a crystal-clear lake mid-scene, and in the background a majestic snow-capped mountain against a cloudless sky. Across that plaque was inscribed the promise from Scripture:
>
> > "I know the plans I have for you," declares the
> > LORD, "plans to prosper you and not to harm
> > you, plans to give you hope and a future."
>
> It is a magnificent biblical promise that is engraved on the photograph of that plaque—in fact, one of my favorite promises of Scripture. But that promise was not made among pine trees and crystal-clear lakes and snow-capped

mountains. Instead, this was a promise made in a city and given . . . to an urban people of God.[1]

After I recovered from shock, I pulled out a Bible and turned to Jeremiah 29. Of course! How could I have missed it? God's promise for the future is for God's people in the city! "For I know the plans I have for you" (29:11) comes just a few verses after, "Seek the peace and prosperity of the city" (29:7). The promises of Jeremiah 29 are for urban exiles.

Having this insight was like coming home. It was as if the Lord was saying, "See? *This* is why I pressed this Scripture into your hearts. I have called you to seek the welfare of the city."

THE CITY OF SATAN

It is not always easy to live, work, or worship in the city. Thomas Jefferson viewed cities "as pestilential to the morals, the health, and the liberties of men."[2] Back in the 1830s the Reverend John Todd warned: "Let no man who values his soul, or his body, ever go into a great city to become a pastor."[3] Todd knew what he was talking about—his church was located in Philadelphia. Ralph Waldo Emerson was even harsher in his infamous judgment: "If all the world was Philadelphia, suicide would be extremely common."

Things were even worse in Babylon. In 597 B.C. King Nebuchadnezzar carried many of the elders, priests, prophets, and people off to Babylon (29:1). Jeremiah's reference to "surviving elders" shows how badly things have gone. The survivors are the lucky ones, so to speak. "This was after King Jehoiachin and the queen mother, the court officials and the leaders of Judah and Jerusalem, the craftsmen and the artisans had gone into exile from Jerusalem" (29:2). The Babylonians have done terrible things to the Jews. They have destroyed their city, ransacked their temple, ruined their economy, removed their leaders, and enslaved their populace.

It is not surprising, then, that Saint Augustine (354-430) viewed Babylon as a symbol of evil. In his classic work *The City of God*, the great African theologian described human history as a conflict between two great cities: the City of God and the City of Man:

> This race we have distributed into two parts, the one consisting of those who live according to man, the other of those who live according to God. And these we also mystically call the two cities, or the two communities of men, of which the one is predestined to reign eternally with God, and the other to suffer eternal punishment with the devil.[4]

Augustine later identified Babylon as the biblical symbol of the city of Satan.

James Montgomery Boice's book *Two Cities, Two Loves* applies Augustine's insights to the post-Christian world:

> According to St. Augustine, who gave us the distinction between "the two cities," . . . Scripture unfolds the history of two distinct groups of people, each having a distinct origin, development, characteristics and destiny. These are two cities or societies. The earthly society has as its highest expression the city cultures of Babylon and . . . Rome. The other is the church, composed of God's elect. The former is destined to pass away. The latter is blessed by God and is to last forever.[5]

To read Jeremiah 29 with the two cities in mind is to recognize that God's people are prisoners in the city of Satan. They are refugees in Babylon, which represents everything hateful and odious to God.

Most postmodern cities are like Babylon. They are Cities of Man ruled by Satan, and Satan is doing his best to turn them into suburbs of hell. One can see it in the abandoned buildings, the graffiti, the tired faces of prostitutes, the racial altercations, the slow shuffle of the poor, and the great buildings built for human pride. Satan has been very busy.

The Dutch Christian Pieter Bos has devoted his life to the city. He was trained as an architect and city planner before becoming a full-time missionary in Amsterdam. This is how he explains the work of Satan in the city:

> In modern cities decisions are often made haphazardly and with no regard for God. As a result, the city falls under the influence of the principalities and powers of Satan. Satan uses the anonymous nature of the city as an environment which encourages the growth of evil. People flock to the cities seduced by the lie that there they will survive. The results are evident in the environment, in the economy, in social problems and in resistance to the gospel.[6]

These problems should concern Christians who do not live in the city as well as those who do. The future of the world is urban. Half the world's population now lives in the city, and the figure will rise to 80 percent during the next half century.[7] The global village is fast becoming a global metropolis.

THE CITY OF GOD

What should God's people do when their zip code places them in Satan's precincts? When God's people were captives in Babylon, they might have expected God to tell them to run away. Or revolt. What he does instead is tell them to make themselves at home. The gist of Jeremiah's prophecy is that God is going to build *his* city in the middle of Satan's city.

Jeremiah was still living back in Jerusalem (29:1), perhaps because the Babylonians did not consider him important enough to deport. Thus, he needed to fax this prophecy to the exiles in

Babylon. (Actually, the letter was written on papyrus and carried in a diplomatic mailbag):

> *"This is what the LORD Almighty, the God of Israel, says to all those I carried into exile from Jerusalem to Babylon: 'Build houses and settle down; plant gardens and eat what they produce. Marry and have sons and daughters; find wives for your sons and give your daughters in marriage, so that they too may have sons and daughters. Increase in number there; do not decrease. Also, seek the peace and prosperity of the city to which I have carried you into exile. Pray to the LORD for it, because if it prospers, you too will prosper.'"* (29:4-7)

God almost sounds like the ad man for Babylonian Realty! Anyone who has tried to buy a house knows how realtors tend to exaggerate. "Charming," the ad will say, which means the house is roughly the size of a telephone booth. "Needs some work" translates as "bring your own wrecking ball." "Luxurious library," I once read on a real estate fact sheet. I imagined myself sitting in a leather armchair at fireside, reading a richly ornamented copy of *Paradise Lost* at the Oxford Union. Then I learned that in the city "luxurious library" means a walk-in closet with bookshelves.

Imagine the reaction when Jeremiah's prophecy is read in the Jewish ghetto in Babylon. There God's people are, languishing in captivity, bemoaning their fate, complaining about the crime and the school system in Babylon. But God gives them the hard sell. "You're going to love this place," he says. "Wonderful place to raise a family! Exciting opportunities for a small business! Great location, right in the heart of the Fertile Crescent!" One senses God's passion for urban planning. Yet he is talking about the city of Babylon, of all places. This is his surprising plan for the redemption of the city. He is going to build the city of God right smack-dab in the middle of the city of Satan.

No doubt when the captives discuss their sojourn in Babylon

they use words like *abandoned* or *banished* or *condemned* to describe what God has done to them. But that is not how God sees things. He views the exile as a mission. Literally, what he says is, "Seek the peace and prosperity of the city to which I have carried you" (29:7). Nebuchadnezzar has not carried them off to Babylon so much as God has sent them there. The exiles are not captives, they are missionaries.

ESTABLISH A PRESENCE IN THE CITY

What has God sent his people to the city to do? First, he has sent them *to establish a presence in the city* (29:5-6). God wants them to get involved in community development. "Build houses and settle down." It almost sounds like a slogan for Habitat for Humanity. God wants to establish a presence in the city, which means living in the city. God's people are resident aliens. Aliens, because they are not living in their home town any more. But also residents, because they live where God wants them to live. Since God has planned for them to have an extended stay, there is no sense renting; they might as well build.

God also wants his people to get involved in agriculture: "Plant gardens and eat what they produce" (29:5). This is a reminder that when God first called Jeremiah, he appointed him "over nations and kingdoms to uproot and tear down, to destroy and overthrow, to build and to plant" (1:10). After twenty-eight chapters of uprooting and overthrowing, Jeremiah is finally getting around to building and planting.

God wants his people to do some matchmaking, maybe start a singles group at the local synagogue: "Marry and have sons and daughters; find wives for your sons and give your daughters in marriage" (29:6a). They should marry off their kids, "so that they too may have sons and daughters. Increase in number there; do not decrease" (29:6b). In short, God wants his people to go about their business as usual. Despite the fact that they are living in a godless city, he wants them to lead normal lives. Furthermore, he wants them to plan for the long haul and build for the future.

These verses teach the importance of daily family life for the redemption of the pagan city. The construction of the house, the planting of the garden, and the raising of the family all build the city of God. The most important thing a Christian parent can do in his or her lifetime is to raise a godly family. And nowhere is the godly family more valuable than in the city.

For some, though not for all, establishing a presence in the city will mean more than just worshiping and ministering in the city. It will mean answering God's call to *live* in the city. For too long, evangelical Christians have abandoned the city to establish the kingdom of God in suburbia. God's plan for the redemption of the city calls Christians to do just the opposite. Ronald J. Sider, who teaches theology at Eastern Baptist Theological Seminary in Philadelphia, argues that,

> Evangelicals must reverse the continuing evangelical flight from the cities. . . . Tens of thousands of evangelicals ought to move back into the city. . . . If one percent of evangelicals living outside the inner city had the faith and courage to move in town, evangelicals would fundamentally alter the history of urban America.[8]

To this it should be added that if one percent of evangelical *families* would move into the city, the impact would be all the greater.

The Lord does not just call people to jobs and to spouses, he also calls them to churches and to cities. I sometimes challenge people to ask the Lord if he is calling them to make a lifetime commitment to Tenth Presbyterian Church. If he is, then I challenge them to ask if God is also calling them to live in the city. When it comes to urban ministry, "being there" makes all the difference:

An outsider can seldom know the needs of the community
well enough to know how best to respond to them. Rarely
if ever can an outsider effectively lead the community in
finding solutions to its own problems. The kind of leader-
ship that empowers people comes from insiders.[9]

Becoming an urban insider was no more popular in
Jeremiah's time than it is in the twentieth and twenty-first centuries. The exiles think their exile will end any minute, so they
still have their bags packed to go back to Jerusalem. They are
working part-time jobs. They are renting rather than buying.
They are not committed to the city. As soon as Jeremiah tells people to settle down in Babylon, he runs into fierce opposition. The
patriots are infuriated. Shemaiah the Nehelamite is so angry he
attacks Jeremiah by way of correspondence. He mails letters—in
his own name, not God's—back to the high priest Zephaniah in
Jerusalem (29:24-25):

> "The LORD has appointed you priest in place of Jehoiada to be
> in charge of the house of the LORD; you should put any mad-
> man who acts like a prophet into the stocks and neck-irons. So
> why have you not reprimanded Jeremiah from Anathoth, who
> poses as a prophet among you? He has sent this message to us
> in Babylon: It will be a long time. Therefore build houses and
> settle down; plant gardens and eat what they produce."
>
> (29:26-28)

Shemaiah understands Jeremiah's message well enough to
summarize it; he just doesn't like it. Since he is sure Jeremiah is
out of his mind, he wants him locked up in the loony bin (cf.
20:2-3). One translation has Shemaiah refer to Jeremiah as that
"crazy fellow who takes himself for a prophet" (29:26).[10] Settle
down in Babylon, you say? You mean, raise a family in the city
of Satan?!

What Shemaiah fails to understand is God's loving plan for

the city. He doesn't understand that, in the words of French social critic Jacques Ellul, the believer's task "is to represent God in the heart of the city."[11]

Fortunately, Zephaniah has the good sense to show his mail to Jeremiah, who knows better than to listen to the propaganda of lying prophets (29:8-9). This is the message Jeremiah sends back to Babylon, *post haste*:

> *"Because Shemaiah has prophesied to you, even though I did not send him, and has led you to believe a lie, this is what the LORD says: I will surely punish Shemaiah the Nehelamite and his descendants. He will have no one left among this people, nor will he see the good things I will do for my people, declares the LORD, because he has preached rebellion against me."*
>
> (29:31-32)

Because Shemaiah is no prophet, he will have no posterity.

Shemaiah's sin was to rebel against God's call to establish a presence in the city. If God calls you to work, worship, or live in the city, do not resist his call. God loves the city. If you love God, then his heart for the city must become your heart for the city.

SEEK THE PEACE OF THE CITY

A second reason God sends his people to the city is *to seek its peace*. Here the *Revised Standard Version* best captures the Hebrew: "Seek the welfare of the city where I have sent you into exile, and pray to the Lord on its behalf, for in its welfare you will find your welfare" (29:7, RSV). The recurrent word for "welfare" is the word *shalom*. Seek the *shalom* of the city; its *shalom* is your *shalom*.

Shalom is comprehensive peace. It means order, health, safety, harmony, well-being, happiness, wholeness, and completeness. *Shalom* means that all is right with the city.

God hereby commands Christians to do anything and everything to further the public good. Seeking the peace of the city means being a good neighbor. It means shoveling the sidewalk. It means cleaning the street. It means planting a tree. It means feeding the poor. It means volunteering at the local school. It means greeting people at the store. It means driving safely and helping people with car trouble. It means shutting down immoral businesses. It means embracing people from every ethnic background with the love of Christ.

Still, a church could do all these things and fail to bring *shalom* to the city. By themselves, random acts of kindness cannot bring a peace that endures. The only basis for real and lasting *shalom* is the work of Christ on the cross. The city cannot be at peace until the city knows Jesus Christ, and him crucified. In its sin, the whole city is at war with God. It deserves the wrath and curse of God. But Jesus Christ came to make peace between God and humanity. The Bible says, "We have peace with God through our Lord Jesus Christ" (Rom. 5:1). Anyone who believes in the Lord Jesus Christ has peace with God.

Whatever *shalom* the Hebrews offered to Babylon, Christians are able to offer a much greater peace to the postmodern city. What we offer is eternal peace with God through the work of Christ on the cross. That peace is the basis for everything else we do in the city. It is what makes us neighborly, compassionate, and charitable. When the city finds peace with God, all will be well with the city.

PRAY FOR THE PROSPERITY OF THE CITY

The last thing God tells his people to do is *to pray for the prosperity of the city*. "Pray to the LORD for it, because if it prospers, you too will prosper" (Jer. 29:7). This is the biblical version of the proverb that a "rising tide lifts all boats." Christians have a vested interest in the welfare of the city. When the city prospers, the church prospers.

That is not how Christians usually think about the city. Many

Christians write the city off. At most, they try to establish their own fortress within the city. But God does not tell his people to seek peace *in* the city; he tells them to seek the peace *of* the city. God is not trying to establish a ghetto, but a government.

One of the best ways to seek the peace of the city is through prayer. Prayer is the Christian's civic duty. It must have been hard for the Jews to pray for the peace of Babylon. The *shalom* of Babylon? It sounds like an oxymoron, a contradiction in terms. Sometimes God's people were even instructed to pray *against* the peace of Babylon:

> O Daughter of Babylon, doomed to destruction,
> happy is he who repays you
>   for what you have done to us—
> he who seizes your infants
>   and dashes them against the rocks. (Ps. 137:8-9)

In fact, Jeremiah 29:7 is the only verse in the entire Old Testament in which God's people are explicitly told to pray for their enemies.[12] Prayer for the Babylonians was a foretaste of the forgiveness of Jesus Christ, who teaches, "Love your enemies and pray for those who persecute you" (Matt. 5:44).

When the Jews in Babylon were at a loss to know how to pray for Babylon, one psalm should have come immediately to mind:

> Pray for peace in Jerusalem:
>   "Prosperity to your houses!
>   Peace inside your city walls!
>   Prosperity to your palaces!"
> Since all are my brothers and friends,
>   I say, "Peace be with you!"
>   Since Yahweh our God lives here,
>   I pray for your happiness. (Ps. 122:6-9, JB)

The language of Jeremiah 29:7 echoes the vocabulary of Psalm 122. The people of God have long prayed for the peace and prosperity of Jerusalem. Now God commands them to use the same liturgy for Babylon.

The same prayer should be offered for the city in these pagan times. Notice four things to pray for.[13] First, pray for the *economy* of the city ("Prosperity to your houses!"). Pray for the "common wealth" of the city, asking God to bring justice to the poor and prosperity for everyone within the economic systems of the city.

Second, pray for the *safety* of the city ("Peace inside your city walls"). Pray that citizens will be kept safe from harm and violence on the streets. And pray that criminals themselves will be transformed by the love of Christ.

Third, pray for the *politics* of the city ("Prosperity to your palaces"). Ask the Lord to grant wisdom and integrity to the authorities who govern the city.

Fourth, pray for the *people* of the city ("Peace be with you"). Pray for the Lord's blessing on all people and all people groups in the city. Pray neighborhood by neighborhood, church by church, business by business, and house by house for the welfare of the city.

Three times a year Christians gather in Center City Philadelphia to take a Prayer Walk in the neighborhood near Tenth Presbyterian Church. We walk the streets of the city asking the Holy Spirit to guide our prayers. We stop at apartment buildings and pray for the salvation of those who live in them. We stop at schools and pray for the teachers. We stop at businesses to pray for their owners. We stop at churches to pray for their ministers. We stop at the street corners and pray for the prostitutes. And we stop at the homes of Christians and pray for their ministry in the city. Prayer should not be kept within the four walls of the church or the home. Get out into the streets to pray for the *shalom* of your neighborhood. The prosperity of the city comes through prayer.

Charles Spurgeon once preached a sermon called "Blessing in the City." It was based on the text, "If thou shalt hearken unto the voice of the Lord thy God. Blessed shalt thou be in the city" (Deut. 28:2-3, KJV). Although Spurgeon's message was meant for a modern city (London) at the dawn of the twentieth century, it is just as appropriate for pagan cities at the dawn of the twenty-first:

> The city is full of care, and he who has to go there from day to day finds it to be a place of great wear and tear. It is full of noise, and stir, and bustle, and sore travail; many are its temptations, losses, and worries. But to go there with the divine blessing takes off the edge of its difficulty; to remain there with that blessing is to find pleasure in its duties, and strength equal to its demands.
>
> A blessing in the city may not make us great, but it will keep us good; it may not make us rich, but it will preserve us honest. Whether we are porters, or clerks, or managers, or merchants, or magistrates, the city will afford us opportunities for usefulness. It is good fishing where there are shoals of fish, and it is hopeful to work for our Lord amid the thronging crowds.

May the Lord bless the city, and the church in the city.

CHAPTER 10

THE NEW
COVENANT

"The time is coming," declares the LORD,
"when I will make a new covenant
with the house of Israel
and with the house of Judah. . . .
I will put my law in their minds
and write it on their hearts.
I will be their God,
and they will be my people. . . .
For I will forgive their wickedness
and will remember their sins no more."

JEREMIAH 31:31, 33B, 34B

A sign in a shop window along Philadelphia's Antique Row reads, "Quality is a thing of the past." The sign is right; newer is not necessarily better. Many new products are flimsy, cheap, and inferior. "The new ones are not as good as the old ones," people say.

Once my mother tried to replace her forty-year-old kitchen faucet because it was starting to corrode. Our plumber counseled against it, saying, "I could give you a new one, but it wouldn't be as good as the old one. They just don't make them like they used to."

Jeremiah 31 ends with the promise of a New Covenant. The promotional material states that it is better than the Old

Covenant. But if quality is a thing of the past, it seems prudent to have a healthy suspicion of all things new. Is the covenant new and improved, or is it just new?

THE OLD COVENANT

God has always dealt with humanity by way of covenant. The *Catechism for Young Children* teaches that a covenant is "An agreement between two or more persons" (Q & A 22). Covenant is often compared to contract, treaty, or alliance.

Many theologians downplay the contractual aspect of biblical covenants. They prefer to think of a covenant as a testament rather than as a bargain. In other words, like a "last will and testament," the blessings of the covenant are bequeathed as free gifts. Thus O. Palmer Robertson calls covenant a "bond in blood sovereignly administered."[1] Similarly, John Murray defines it as "a sovereign administration of grace and of promise."[2]

Even a gracious covenant, however, calls for a response on the part of God's people. For this reason, Robert Davidson says that covenant is "a relationship rooted in God's initiative, in what he has done *for* the people, but it looks for a response *from* the people."[3] The classic covenant theologian Herman Witsius (1636-1708) also highlights our human responsibility to respond to God's grace:

> A covenant of God with man, is an agreement between God and man, about the way of obtaining consummate happiness; including a commination of eternal destruction, with which the contemner of the happiness, offered in that way, is to be punished.[4]

Perhaps a shorter definition is possible: A biblical covenant is a binding relationship in which God promises to bless and his people promise to obey.

The history of God's people is a story of covenants. In the

covenant of works Adam was bound to obey God perfectly. For his part, God promised to reward Adam with life if he obeyed and threatened to punish Adam with death if he disobeyed (Gen. 2:16-17).

God made a covenant of safety with Noah and every living creature (Gen. 9:8-17). The rainbow is a sign of God's covenant promise that he will never again destroy the world with a flood.

God made a covenant of destiny with Abraham (Gen. 12:1-3; 15:1-21; 17:1-27). He promised to give him a land populated with descendants as numerous as the stars (Gen. 15:5). God said, "This is my covenant with you: You will be the father of many nations. . . . I will establish my covenant as an everlasting covenant between me and you and your descendants after you" (Gen. 17:4, 7). He also promised that through Abraham's "offspring all nations on earth will be blessed" (Gen. 22:18; cf. 12:3). For his part, Abraham was bound to obey God by circumcising every male in his household (Gen. 17:9-14). Every one of these covenants was a personal bond in which God promised to bless and his people promised to obey.

In Jeremiah 31 God refers to the "the covenant I made with their forefathers when I took them by the hand to lead them out of Egypt" (Jer. 31:32). For Jeremiah, therefore, the Old Covenant means the covenant God made with his people at Mount Sinai. The Mosaic Covenant was for a people already saved by grace. "God spoke all these words: 'I am the LORD your God, who brought you out of Egypt, out of the land of slavery'" (Ex. 20:1-2). Once they were saved, God's people had to keep God's covenant in order to receive God's blessing. They were bound to worship God alone, keep the Sabbath holy, preserve the sanctity of human life, tell the truth, and obey the rest of the Ten Commandments (Ex. 20:3-17). The Mosaic Covenant was a good and gracious covenant.

THE BROKEN COVENANT

There was only one problem with the Old Covenant: Sin. The covenant was broken even before it could be ratified. By the time Moses came down from the mountain, the people had cast a golden idol in the shape of a calf. "When Moses approached the camp and saw the calf and the dancing, his anger burned and he threw the tablets out of his hands, breaking them to pieces at the foot of the mountain" (Ex. 32:19).

So God re-issued the covenant (Ex. 34), only to see his people break it all over again. The history of the Old Testament is one of idolatry, immorality, discontent, and disobedience. According to Old Testament scholar Gerhard Von Rad, "The reason why a new covenant is to ensue on the old is not that the regulations revealed in the latter have proved inadequate, but that the covenant has been broken, because Israel has refused to obey it."[5] J. A. Thompson goes one step further: "They had not merely refused to obey the law or to acknowledge Yahweh's complete and sole sovereignty, but were incapable of such obedience."[6]

Jeremiah rightly identifies sin as the problem with the Old Covenant. "'They broke my covenant, though I was a husband to them,' declares the LORD" (Jer. 31:32). "Jeremiah does not condemn the old covenant. He condemns Israel for breaking the covenant."[7] And not just breaking it. The first twenty-eight chapters of Jeremiah are an exhaustive record of how Judah shattered the covenant and ground the fragments into dust.

The shocking thing is that this agreement was actually a marriage covenant. More than once Jeremiah states that God is like a husband to his people. But the day has finally come when God files for divorce. The first chapter of this book recounted how God took Israel to divorce court. Israel "fell out of love" and committed spiritual adultery "on every high hill and under every spreading tree" (2:20b). Israel stood up in court to deny the charges, but God made them stick. God's virgin bride had become a spiritual whore.

Here is the real shocker, however: If every sin is an act of covenant-breaking, then every sinner is a covenant-breaker. Every time you sin, you are being unfaithful in your marriage to God. That is why sin is so tawdry, cheap, and degrading. As the apostle Paul so carefully explained, there is nothing wrong with the law, the commandment, or the Old Covenant (Rom. 7:7-13). The problem is with us. We are covenant-breakers by nature.

Failure to keep covenant brings a curse (cf. Jer. 11:8, 10-11). Jeremiah cites the conventional wisdom of his day: "The fathers have eaten sour grapes, and the children's teeth are set on edge" (Jer. 31:29). This must have been a popular saying because the prophet Ezekiel also quotes it (Ezek. 18:2). It is a memorable proverb. When a father bites into an unripe grape, the lips of his children pucker in disgust. This refers to the curse of the Old Covenant, in which God threatened to punish "the children for the sin of the fathers to the third and fourth generation" (Ex. 20:5).

How the people of Judah resented that curse! "While in exile the people concluded out of self-pity and fatalistic despair that they were being punished unjustly for sins of previous genera-tions."[8] They felt sorry for themselves. The sour grapes their fathers ate had left a bitter taste in their mouths. Why should they suffer for the spiritual adultery of their parents?

Jeremiah teaches that people deserve God's curse for their own sins as well as for their parents' sins. "Everyone will die for his own sin; whoever eats sour grapes—his own teeth will be set on edge" (Jer. 31:30). Corporately or individually, everyone who breaks covenant is under God's curse. This is also true for nations—like the United States of America—that have covenanted to live under God.

THE NEW COVENANT

If the Old Covenant ends in a curse, then the New Covenant merits investigation. Jeremiah 31 is the place to start because it is the only passage in the Old Testament that promises a "new covenant." It is the one place in the Old Covenant that lists all the promises of the New Covenant. And since a covenant is also called a "testament," it is the passage that gives the New Testament its name.

There are seven promises in all. First, the New Covenant holds the promise of *reconciliation*. It will bring all God's people together into one redeemed race:

> *"The time is coming," declares the LORD,*
> *"when I will make a new covenant*
> *with the house of Israel*
> *and with the house of Judah."* (31:31)

Because of its emphasis on personal responsibility, Jeremiah's New Covenant is sometimes viewed as the triumph of individualism. R. K. Harrison says,

> Probably the most significant contribution which Jeremiah made to religious thought was inherent in his insistence that the new covenant involved a one-to-one relationship of the spirit. When the new covenant was inaugurated by the atoning work of Jesus Christ on Calvary, this important development of personal, as opposed to corporate, faith and spirituality was made real for the whole of mankind.[9]

The trouble with this view is that the first promise of the New Covenant is a corporate promise, not an individual promise. The New Covenant will end the division between the tribes of Israel in the north and the tribes of Judah in the south. God will plant both houses in one land (31:27).

Jeremiah first issued the promise of reconciliation at the beginning of his book:

> At that time they will call Jerusalem The Throne of the LORD, and all nations will gather in Jerusalem to honor the name of the LORD. No longer will they follow the stubbornness of their evil hearts. In those days the house of Judah will join the house of Israel, and together they will come from a northern land to the land I gave your forefathers as an inheritance. (3:17-18)

He will repeat the promise at the end of his book:

> "In those days, at that time,"
>   declares the LORD,
> "the people of Israel and the people of Judah together
>   will go in tears to seek the LORD their God.
> They will ask the way to Zion
>   and turn their faces toward it.
> They will come and bind themselves to the LORD
>   in an everlasting covenant
>   that will not be forgotten." (50:4-5)

Jeremiah's promises were fulfilled with the coming of Christ. There is only one New Covenant people of God. "There is neither Jew nor Greek, slave nor free, male nor female, for you are all one in Christ Jesus" (Gal. 3:28). In the New Covenant community there is no black, no white, no brown. There is no rich and no poor, only one New Covenant people in Christ.

Second, the New Covenant is a covenant of *regeneration*. It will transform God's people from the inside out:

> "This is the covenant I will make with the house of Israel
>   after that time," declares the LORD.
> "I will put my law in their minds
>   and write it on their hearts." (Jer. 31:33)

The problem with the Mosaic Covenant was that it was written on tablets of stone (Ex. 31:18). If anything was written on the hearts of God's people, it was only their sin:

> *"Judah's sin is engraved with an iron tool,*
> *   inscribed with a flint point,*
> *   on the tablets of their hearts."* (Jer. 17:1; cf. 17:9)

In the New Covenant, however, God solves the problem of the sinful heart by giving his children new hearts and new minds. According to Calvin, the New Covenant "penetrates into the heart and reforms all the inward faculties, so that obedience is rendered to the righteousness of God."[10]

It must be emphasized that the New Covenant does not abolish the Old. Christ did not come to abolish the law, but to fulfill it (Matt. 5:17). Thus, "the *new* covenant is not so called because it is contrary to the first covenant."[11] Both covenants demand obedience to the law. The difference is that the New Covenant brings the law from the outside to the inside. "The distinctiveness of the ministry of law under the New Covenant resides in its inward character. Rather than being administered externally, the law shall be administered from within the heart."[12]

Thomas à Kempis (c. 1380-1471) wrote a beautiful prayer about his longing for a new heart:

> *Write your blessed name, O Lord, upon my heart,*
> *There to remain so indelibly engraved*
> *   that no prosperity or adversity*
> *shall ever remove me from your love.*
> *   O Jesu, my only Savior!*
> *Write your blessed name, O Lord, upon my heart.*[13]

The law written on the heart is a promise about the coming of the Holy Spirit, for Hebrews attributes Jeremiah's promise to the Holy Spirit:

The Holy Spirit also testifies to us about this. First he says:
"This is the covenant I will make with them
after that time, says the Lord.
I will put my laws in their hearts,
and I will write them on their minds." (Heb. 10:15-16)

Only the Holy Spirit can change a heart. A sinner whose heart has been regenerated by God's Spirit knows how to please God. He or she does not need to pull out a Bible every time a decision needs to be made. The law written on the heart helps the Christian know what to do instantly and instinctively.

For the Christian, obedience to the law is not a prior condition for entering the New Covenant. Rather, it is one of the promised blessings of the New Covenant. In his personal notes on this verse Jonathan Edwards (1703-1758) wrote:

> I think the difference here pointed out between these two covenants, lies plainly here, that in the old covenant God promised to be their God upon condition of hearty obedience; obedience was stipulated as a condition, but not promised. But in the new covenant, this hearty obedience is promised.[14]

Third, the New Covenant is a covenant of *possession*. God's people have a claim on God and he has a claim on them. "I will be their God, and they will be my people" (Jer. 31:33b; cf. 7:23; 11:4; 24:7; 30:22; 31:1; 32:38). God's people are no longer their own. They belong to God and God belongs to them

The promise of belonging to God in a mutual love relationship is among the most frequently repeated promises of the Old Testament:

"I will take you as my own people, and I will be your God."
                                                              (Ex. 6:7)

> *You have declared this day that the* LORD *is your God and*
> *that you will walk in his ways, that you will keep his decrees,*
> *commands and laws, and that you will obey him. And the*
> LORD *has declared this day that you are his people, his trea-*
> *sured possession as he promised, and that you are to keep*
> *all his commands.*
> (Deut. 26:17-18; cf. 29:12-13; Ezek. 11:20)

> *"My beloved is mine, and I am his."* (Song 2:16a; KJV)

> *"I will say to those called 'Not my people,' 'You are my peo-*
> *ple'; and they will say, 'You are my God.'"*
> (Hos. 2:23b; cf. Zech. 8:8)

Whenever God makes a covenant with his people, what he is really giving them is himself. The primary blessing of the New Covenant is friendship and fellowship with the Triune God. This "is the crown and goal of the whole process of religion, namely, union and communion with God."[15]

THE NEW COVENANT CONTINUED

Fourth, the New Covenant will complete the task of *evangelization*:

> *"No longer will a man teach his neighbor,*
> *or a man his brother, saying, 'Know the* LORD,'
> *because they will all know me,*
> *from the least of them to the greatest,"*
> *declares the* LORD. (Jer. 31:34)

The Bible often commands believers to teach one another to know the Lord (Deut. 6:1-9; Col. 3:16). But the day will come when such teaching will no longer be necessary. Everyone—from the youngest babe to the oldest saint—will know God. Here the word *know* "carries its most profound connotation, the intimate personal knowledge which arises between two persons who are committed wholly to one another in a relationship that touches mind, emotion, and will."[16]

To a limited degree, this promise has already come true in the church. Every believer knows Jesus Christ. So although every Christian needs the Gospel every day, every Christian does not need to be converted every day.

Yet the promise of the end of evangelization is especially for eternity. There will be no revival meetings in heaven. No one will stand on the corner and pass out tracts. No one will share the Four Spiritual Laws. No one will knock on your door and ask, "If you were to die tonight, what would you say to God when he asks, 'Why should I let you into my heaven?'" There will be no evangelism because there will be no need. Everyone will know God, from the least to the greatest.

Fifth, the New Covenant will be a covenant of *satisfaction for sin*. "For I will forgive their wickedness and will remember their sins no more" (Jer. 31:34). This is perhaps the best blessing of the New Covenant. The Old Covenant tried to deal with the problem of sin through the sacrifices of the law. But in the New Covenant God deals with sin once and for all. The price for sin will be paid in full. God not only forgives, he forgets.

The way the New Covenant deals with the problem of sin is through the death of Jesus Christ on the cross. The sins of God's people were forgiven and forgotten at Calvary. When Jesus celebrated Passover with his disciples, "He took the cup, saying, 'This cup is the new covenant in my blood, which is poured out for you'" (Luke 22:20; cf. 1 Cor. 11:25). Jesus was claiming that all the promises of the New Covenant find their fulfillment in him. Jesus *is* the New Covenant. The New Covenant is established by his blood shed on the cross for sins. All the blessings of the New Covenant are located in the crucified (and risen!) Christ.

The writer to the Hebrews was captivated by Jeremiah's

vision of the New Covenant. Again and again, he speaks of "a better covenant" (Heb. 7:22) or a "superior covenant founded on better promises" (Heb. 8:6). A better covenant was needed because there was a problem with the old one. It was the same problem Jeremiah identified: "For if there had been nothing wrong with that first covenant, no place would have been sought for another. But God found fault with the people" (Heb. 8:7-8a). God found fault—not with the covenant—but with the people. A better covenant was needed to deal with the problem of sin.

The better covenant in Hebrews is one and the same as the New Covenant in Jeremiah, for Hebrews quotes Jeremiah's entire promise (Heb. 8:8-12). Then the writer to the Hebrews makes this statement: "By calling this covenant 'new,' he [God] has made the first one obsolete" (Heb. 8:13a). We have already seen that the Old Covenant is not abolished but fulfilled in the New. The laws of the Old Covenant remain, now written on the heart. But the New Covenant is so much better that it is as if the Old has been done away with completely.

The reason the New Covenant is so much better is because, "Christ is the mediator of a new covenant, that those who are called may receive the promised eternal inheritance—now that he has died as a ransom to set them free from the sins committed under the first covenant" (Heb. 9:15; cf. Heb. 12:24). The New Covenant offers full and final satisfaction for the curse of God against every kind of covenant-breaking.

Sixth, the New Covenant will be endless in *duration*:

> This is what the LORD says,
> he who appoints the sun to shine by day,
> who decrees the moon and stars to shine by night,
> who stirs up the sea so that its waves roar—
>   the LORD Almighty is his name:
> "Only if these decrees vanish from my sight,"
>   declares the LORD,

"will the descendants of Israel ever cease
to be a nation before me."
This is what the LORD *says:*
"Only if the heavens above can be measured
and the foundations of the earth below be searched out
will I reject all the descendants of Israel
because of all they have done,"
declares the LORD. (Jer. 31:35-37)

The God of creation is also the God of salvation. Therefore, the New Covenant in Christ is as reliable as the fixed laws of nature, if not more so. It is irrevocable.

Jeremiah's pleas for God to remember his covenant have not gone unanswered (14:21). Not even the disastrous events of 587 B.C. (the ultimate fall of Jerusalem and the beginning of the Babylonian captivity) will mark its end. The New Covenant is as likely to fail as the entire universe is to grind to a halt. God will no more forget his people than humanity will unravel all the mysteries of interstellar space. The New Covenant is an everlasting covenant.

Theologians have struggled to explain the eternal duration of the covenant. The biblical covenants often sound like contracts, as if God does his part and we do our part. But of course we never keep our end of the bargain, so the covenant ought to be null and void. Yet the mystery of God's grace is that he continues to keep covenant even when we break it.

The only explanation for the permanence of the covenant is that Jesus Christ keeps it on our behalf. His covenant-keeping counts for us. The *Westminster Larger Catechism* asks, "With whom was the covenant of grace made?" Answer: "The covenant of grace was made with Christ as the second Adam, and in him with all the elect as his seed" (Q & A 30). In other words, the New Covenant is not a bargain between God and us. If that were the case, the New Covenant would be no better than the

Old. Rather, the New Covenant is a blood bond between God the Father and God the Son on our behalf. Jesus Christ makes and keeps the covenant for us. We are in the covenant because we are in Christ.

Seventh, the New Covenant is a covenant of *urbanization*:

> *"The days are coming," declares the LORD, "when this city will be rebuilt for me from the Tower of Hananel to the Corner Gate. The measuring line will stretch from there straight to the hill of Gareb and then turn to Goah. The whole valley where dead bodies and ashes are thrown, and all the terraces out to the Kidron Valley on the east as far as the corner of the Horse Gate, will be holy to the LORD. The city will never again be uprooted or demolished." (31:38-40)*

Jeremiah's first calling was "to uproot and tear down, and to overthrow, destroy and bring disaster" (31:28; cf. 1:10). After forty years of demolition work, his prophecies have all come true. The Babylonians have uprooted, torn down, overthrown, and destroyed Jerusalem.

Now Jeremiah enters the second phase of his ministry. The time has come for God "to build and to plant" (31:28; cf. 1:10). This is a promise of urban renewal. As Jeremiah goes on a grand tour of the city, he notes its landmarks and describes its boundaries. He is making real promises for a real city. There will be life after death for Jerusalem. The parts of the city that lie in ruins will be rebuilt. What has been cursed will be blessed. The profane will be made sacred. Even the Valley of Ben Hinnom—the Auschwitz of ancient Palestine where children were cremated on pagan altars (7:30-32)—will become "holy to the Lord" (31:40). The graveyard and the garbage dump will become holy ground.

All these promises came true. When Nehemiah rebuilt Jerusalem after the exile, his engineers started at "the Tower of Hananel" (Neh. 3:1) and worked their way around Jeremiah's map to make repairs "above the Horse Gate" (3:28). That was the earthly, physical fulfillment of Jeremiah's promise.

There is also a heavenly, spiritual fulfillment of the urban promise of the New Covenant. God is building his people an eternal city. In the words of Oxford theologian Oliver O'Donovan, "No destiny can possibly be conceived in the world, or even out of it, other than that of a city."[17] When Christ returns, his people will see "the Holy City, the new Jerusalem, coming down out of heaven from God" (Rev. 21:2).

IN THE COVENANT

Bible expositions often end by applying the promises and commands of God to daily life. But after hearing the seven promises of the New Covenant, what still needs to be done?

There is nothing left to do, only believe. For all the promises of the New Covenant are things God undertakes: "I will make a new covenant" (Jer. 31:31); "I will put my law in their minds. . . . I will be their God" (31:33); "I will forgive their wickedness" (31:34); "[I will not] reject all the descendants of Israel" (31:37). All the terms of the New Covenant are promises. As the great covenant theologian Thomas Boston (1676-1732) taught,

> What remains for sinners, that they may be personally and savingly in covenant with God, is not, as parties, contractors and undertakers, to make a covenant with him for life and salvation; but only, to take hold of God's covenant already made from eternity, between the Father and Christ the second Adam, and revealed and offered to us in the gospel.[18]

CHAPTER 11

BUYER'S MARKET

"Then, just as the LORD had said, my cousin Hanamel came to me in the courtyard of the guard and said, 'Buy my field at Anathoth in the territory of Benjamin. Since it is your right to redeem it and possess it, buy it for yourself.' I knew that this was the word of the LORD; so I bought the field at Anathoth from my cousin Hanamel and weighed out for him seventeen shekels of silver."

JEREMIAH 32:8-9

Some years after he reported God's promise of a New Covenant, Jeremiah's faith is tested. God tells him to buy a piece of property, even though buying it would seem to be a complete waste of money.

The real estate principle that applies to Jeremiah's purchase is known as anticipation:

According to the principle of *anticipation*, property value may be affected by expectation of a future event. . . . Real estate has historically proved to be a generally appreciating asset. . . . However, anticipation may also lower value if property rights are expected to be restricted or if the property somehow becomes less appealing to prospective buyers.[1]

In other words, how much a piece of real estate is worth depends on what is expected to happen to it in the future. If the government decides to run a superhighway through your dining room, for example, your property value will plummet.

A BAD TIME TO BUY

The principle of anticipation helps explain why Jeremiah's land deal seems like such a bad investment. It is absolutely the worst time for Jeremiah to buy. At the time God tells him to buy the property, Jeremiah is "confined in the courtyard of the guard in the royal palace of Judah" (32:2b). It would certainly seem like a bad time to invest in real estate, especially out in the countryside. Even if the prophet buys the ranch, he will be unable to farm it.

Jeremiah has been sent to jail by the king himself:

> *Now Zedekiah king of Judah had him imprisoned there, saying, "Why do you prophesy as you do? You say, 'This is what the LORD says: I am about to hand this city over to the king of Babylon, and he will capture it. Zedekiah king of Judah will not escape out of the hands of the Babylonians but will certainly be handed over to the king of Babylon, and will speak with him face to face and see him with his own eyes. He will take Zedekiah to Babylon, where he will remain until I deal with him, declares the LORD. If you fight against the Babylonians, you will not succeed.'"* (32:3-5)

It is not hard to understand Zedekiah's anger. Jeremiah has prophesied that the king will be defeated and humiliated. At best, his words are demoralizing; at worst, they are treason (cf. chapters 37—38). Thus, Jeremiah's life is in Zedekiah's hands. And buying *a* farm becomes less appealing when there is a good chance of buying *the* farm.

Then there is the war. As it says in the real estate textbooks, "Anticipation may also lower value if property rights are expected to be restricted or if the property somehow becomes less appealing to prospective buyers." Less appealing? Restricted? Jeremiah's settlement on this property will take place "in the tenth year of Zedekiah king of Judah" (32:1). In other words, it will take place in 587 B.C., the year "the army of the king of Babylon was . . . besieging Jerusalem" (32:2). In a matter of months the city will be destroyed by the Babylonians.

During the last days before the fall of Jerusalem, the bottom will fall out of the housing market. Things will get so bad that entire houses and palaces will be torn down in a desperate attempt to shore up the city walls (33:4). It hardly seems like the time to buy. Imagine trying to persuade a bank to give you a loan when your city is surrounded by the most powerful army on earth.

In short, this is positively the worst time for Jeremiah to buy. "The city is under siege, and the prophet is under arrest."[2]

A LONG LOST COUSIN

Then Hanamel shows up to visit Jeremiah in prison. Long-lost cousin Hanamel is one of the great characters and all-time wheeler-dealers of the Old Testament. There is someone like Hanamel in most families. He is the cousin everyone avoids at family reunions because he is always trying to sell something. He hasn't been seen or heard from in years, but he slaps everyone on the back and says, "Listen, have I got a sweetheart of a deal for you! It's a once-in-a-lifetime opportunity!"

It is kind of God to warn Jeremiah that Hanamel is coming (32:7). Jeremiah probably needs some time to brace himself:

> *"Then, just as the LORD had said, my cousin Hanamel came to me in the courtyard of the guard and said, 'Buy my field at Anathoth in the territory of Benjamin. Since it is your right to redeem it and possess it, buy it for yourself.'"* (32:8)

The Bible does not say why Hanamel is giving Jeremiah the option to buy. Maybe he is trying to make a fast shekel before the Babylonians take over. Perhaps he is in debt and needs the money to buy food. In any case, he appeals to the prophet's sense of family obligation. According to the law of Moses (Lev. 25:25-34), the Promised Land is a sacred inheritance. Property is not to leave the family. God does not want his people to go outside their bloodlines to get help. If they fall into debt, one of their own kin is supposed to redeem their property. Hanamel is asking Jeremiah to be his kinsman redeemer (*goel*; cf. Ruth 4:1-12).

No doubt Jeremiah's realtor would have counseled against accepting the offer. The old family farm is on the outskirts of Jerusalem, in Anathoth (cf. Jer. 1:1), which at this very moment is enemy-occupied territory. To put it bluntly, it is a dumb time to buy.

But Jeremiah buys the land anyway. He conducts the settlement by the book. He scrapes together the money for a down payment, looks over the terms of the contract, signs the deed, has it notarized, and takes it to the title office. Duplicate copies are made, one open for inspection and one sealed in case of a later dispute:

> "I bought the field at Anathoth from my cousin Hanamel and weighed out for him seventeen shekels of silver. I signed and sealed the deed, had it witnessed, and weighed out the silver on the scales. I took the deed of purchase—the sealed copy containing the terms and conditions, as well as the unsealed copy— and I gave this deed to Baruch son of Neriah, the son of Mahseiah, in the presence of my cousin Hanamel and of the witnesses who had signed the deed and of all the Jews sitting in the courtyard of the guard." (32:9-12)

This is more or less how real estate transactions are settled to this very day, which is a reminder that the people of the Bible lived in the real world. Then, as now, buying property was too important to rely on a handshake.

A GOOD REASON TO BUY

Once Jeremiah signs the deed, Hanamel probably laughs all the way to the bank. At first he couldn't even give the property away, but somehow he has managed to persuade Jeremiah to pay him seventeen shekels for it. It is not a large sum of money, but Hanamel is happy to take whatever he can get. The deed probably is not even worth the papyrus it is scratched on. Any price is too much to pay for a property under Babylonian occupation, purchased sight-unseen. "The Prophet must have appeared to have been beside himself when he bought a field in the possession of enemies."[3]

So why did Jeremiah do it? For one thing, because the Lord told him to, which is the best reason to do anything. In the prophet's own words: "I knew that this was the word of the LORD; so I bought the field at Anathoth from my cousin Hanamel" (32:8b-9). But there was more to the deal than sheer obedience.

A similar purchase was made several centuries later, during the Second Punic War (between Carthage and Rome, 218-202 B.C.). Livy, the Roman historian, writes how Hannibal, the North African general, sailed across the Straits of Gibraltar, conquered Spain, crossed the Alps with his elephants and marched on the city of Rome. It happened that when Hannibal arrived on the outskirts of Rome, the very piece of property on which he was camped came up for sale by auction. It was purchased by a Roman citizen "without any reduction in price." When Hannibal heard about it, he was outraged. Livy writes, "That a purchaser should have been found in Rome for the land he had taken by force of arms and of which he was now the occupier and owner seemed to him evidence of outrageous conceit."[4]

Jeremiah makes the same kind of purchase, but not from outrageous conceit. Rather, it is audacious faith that leads him to pay
full market value. "For this is what the LORD Almighty, the God
of Israel, says: Houses, fields and vineyards will again be bought
in this land" (32:15). It may be a bad time to buy, but Jeremiah
has good reason to buy. Eventually, God is going to bring his people back home from their exile. Property values will go back up.
Despite the war, the siege, the destruction the Babylonians are
about to wreak on Jerusalem, and the seventy long years of captivity that will ensue, it is a buyer's market for those who trust
God's promises.

Jeremiah believes. He is willing to take the long view. He tells
his secretary to put his title in a safe deposit box:

> "In their presence I gave Baruch these instructions: 'This is
> what the LORD Almighty, the God of Israel, says: Take these
> documents, both the sealed and unsealed copies of the deed of
> purchase, and put them in a clay jar so they will last a long
> time.'" (32:13-14)

This was standard practice for keeping a document safe in
those days. It was a good system: For two millennia, the famous
Dead Sea Scrolls were protected by clay jars in the caves at
Qumran. The Shrine of the Book, the museum in Jerusalem
where some of those scrolls are now housed, also exhibits property deeds like the ones Jeremiah's secretary held for Hanamel's
property.

Preserving the title to the property was an act of faith. When
Jeremiah signed and sealed the deed, he was banking on God's
ability to deliver on his promises. By faith, he was making an
investment in the kingdom of God. Derek Kidner observes: "To
buy land overrun by the world's conqueror, and then to take elab-
orate care of the title deeds was a striking affirmation, as solid as
the silver that paid for it, that God would bring his people back

to their inheritance."[5] Even though Jeremiah would not live to see that day, he made sure the documents would be around to prove that God was faithful to his promise.

Do you have faith to act on God's promises, even if some of them will not be fulfilled until the end of history? Jeremiah had that kind of faith. He made a major life decision based on what God promised to do seven decades later.

Christians make the same kinds of decisions every day. They do strange things because they trust the promises of God. Some Christians get married. How odd! With the divorce rate so high, why would anyone want to get married? Christians get married because God tells them to do it and because they trust his faithfulness for the future.

Some Christians raise families. This, too, is becoming increasingly radical. A Christian woman went to see her dentist, whose wife was expecting a baby. The patient told him how wonderful it was to raise children. Afterwards, the dental hygienist told her she could tell whether or not people were Christians by what they said to the dentist about having a baby. Non-Christians talked about what a nuisance it is to have children, but Christians viewed them as a gift from the Lord.

Some Christians go to faraway lands as missionaries, which is even stranger than raising a family. They leave behind all the conveniences of American culture. Why on earth would anyone do that? They do it because God has called them to take the Gospel to the ends of the earth, and because they trust his promise that he will go with them (Matt. 28:18).

The list goes on and on. Some Christians move into the city. On purpose. Some Christians feed the homeless or tutor the ignorant. Some Christians reach across ethnic and economic barriers to form friendships. Some Christians give up one night a week to study the Bible and pray in small groups. Some Christians give away 10 percent of their income—or more—for the work of the church.

All these behaviors seem strange to the pagan mind. The strongest countercultural movement in twenty-first century America will be the church of the Lord Jesus Christ. There will only be one good explanation for the strange things Christians do: They believe the promises of God. They trust what God has said about the family, or evangelism, or compassion, or stewardship, and they act accordingly.

A PRAYER FOR THE BEWILDERED

Living for God was as daunting a challenge in Jeremiah's times as it is in our own. As soon as the prophet has put his money where his mouth is, he turns to the Lord in prayer: "After I had given the deed of purchase to Baruch son of Neriah, I prayed to the LORD" (Jer. 32:16). Calvin observes that "by this we are taught, that whenever thoughts creep into our minds, which toss us here and there, we ought to flee to prayer."[6]

What follows is a page from Jeremiah's prayer journal. It is a prayer for the bewildered. For forty years Jeremiah has preached the destruction of Jerusalem. But when the city is finally about to be overrun, God tells him to buy land. Jeremiah obeys the Lord immediately, of course, but then he has second thoughts. So he takes his doubts and his misgivings to the Lord in prayer. Derek Kidner says:

> It is a fine example of the way to pray in a desperate situation: concentrating first on the creative power (17) and perfect fidelity and justice (18-19) of God; remembering next his great redemptive acts (20-23a; to which the Christian can now add the greatest of them all)—and then with this background, laying before God the guilt of the past (23b), the hard facts of the present (24) and the riddle of the future (25).[7]

There are four parts to Jeremiah's prayer. The first is the

groan. "Ah!" says Jeremiah, or "Alas!" He begins his prayer with a cry from the soul.

Jeremiah often did this when he was in distress. Four of his prayers begin, not with a word, but with an "Ah!" When God called him to the ministry, Jeremiah prayed: "'Ah, Sovereign LORD,' I said, 'I do not know how to speak; I am only a child'" (Jer. 1:6). When the Lord announced that Jerusalem would be invaded, Jeremiah said, "Ah, Sovereign LORD, how completely you have deceived this people and Jerusalem by saying, 'You will have peace,' when the sword is at our throats" (4:10). He prayed the same way when the other clergy were speaking against him. "I said, 'Ah, Sovereign LORD, the prophets keep telling them, "You will not see the sword or suffer famine. Indeed, I will give you lasting peace in this place"'" (14:13).

Whenever Jeremiah had a crisis—whenever he did not know what the Lord wanted him to do, was worried about the future, or was being attacked by enemies—his soul cried out to the Lord. Thus, he experienced the truth of this wonderful New Testament promise:

> *The Spirit helps us in our weakness. We do not know what we ought to pray for, but the Spirit himself intercedes for us with groans that words cannot express. And he who searches our hearts knows the mind of the Spirit, because the Spirit intercedes for the saints in accordance with God's will.*
>
> (Rom. 8:26-27)

It is appropriate to begin some prayers with a groan. When the only thing that comes out is "Arrrgh!" God knows what you mean. The Holy Spirit articulates the cries of the soul. He turns groaning into intercession.

Second, Jeremiah praises God for his mighty acts: "Great are your purposes and mighty are your deeds" (Jer. 32:19a). He starts with God's mighty act of Creation. "Ah, Sovereign LORD, you have made the heavens and the earth by your great power and outstretched arm" (32:17a). The Lord God made everything there is. He made "the heavens and the earth," which is another way of saying he made the entire universe. He made all the moons, stars, planets, and galaxies. He made all the birds, bugs, and beasts. He made all the trees, bushes, flowers, and plants. Without God nothing was made that has been made.

The Christian doctrine of Creation stands against the philosophy of naturalism. Naturalism is one of the dominant worldviews of pagan culture. It is the belief—notice the word *belief*—that nature is all there is. There is no God, no soul, and no spirit, only matter in motion.

Since the days of Charles Darwin (1809-1882), naturalism has told its own creation story. The Harvard paleontologist George Gaylord Simpson puts it like this: "Man is the result of a purposeless and natural process that did not have him in mind."[8] In other words, the existence of human beings is an accident, the product of chance.

In his critique of naturalism, University of California at Berkeley professor Phillip Johnson points out that naturalism reverses the biblical doctrine of creation.[9] If the Bible is true, then God created mankind. But if naturalism is true, then mankind created God. God is just make-believe. He does not actually exist; he is a product of the human mind.

Naturalism thus denies God his proper place of rule over the universe. It denies him the worship and the praise that rightfully belong to him as the Creator of all that is. When God is praised for his mighty acts of Creation, he is put back in his proper place. And his worshipers put themselves back in their proper place. God is the Creator; we are creatures God made by his "great power and outstretched arm" (32:17).

The other mighty act Jeremiah mentions is redemption (32:20-23). He gives a short history lesson about how God brought his people out of Egypt. "You performed miraculous signs and wonders in Egypt and have continued them to this day, both in Israel and among all mankind, and have gained the renown that is still yours" (32:20). Jeremiah has in mind the miracles of Moses and the plagues on the Egyptians. He remembers that God not only brought his people out of Egypt, he also brought them into Canaan, the Promised Land, "a land flowing with milk and honey" (32:22). Again, God did all this "by a mighty hand and an outstretched arm" (32:21).

God is to be praised as both Creator and Redeemer. When the Christian praises God as Redeemer, he praises God for salvation in Jesus Christ. Calvin emphasized this by the way he organized his *Institutes*.[10] The first book concerns "the Knowledge of God the Creator." The second teaches "the Knowledge of God the Redeemer in Christ." To redeem is to purchase or to buy back. God has redeemed his people from sin and death through the death and resurrection of Jesus Christ. "In him we have redemption through his blood, the forgiveness of sins" (Eph. 1:7-8). Anyone who is made in the image of God can praise God as Creator. But everyone who believes in Jesus Christ for salvation can also praise him as Redeemer.

Third, Jeremiah worships God for his glorious attributes. He does not praise him simply for what he does, but also for who he is. He crams as many of God's characteristics as possible into two and a half verses.

He starts with God's omnipotence. "Nothing is too hard for you" (Jer. 32:17b). Whatever the task, God is up to it. He never meets his limitations. Nothing is too difficult for him.

Next Jeremiah worships God for his covenant love. "You show love to thousands" (32:18). Thousands upon millions of believers have been showered with the love of God in Christ, throughout history and around the globe. Jeremiah's "love to thousands" echoes the second commandment, which speaks of God "showing love to a thousand generations" of those who love him and keep his commandments (Ex. 20:6; cf. Ex. 34:6-7).

Jeremiah also echoes the second commandment when he praises God for his justice. "You . . . bring the punishment for the fathers' sins into the laps of their children" (Jer. 32:18). Or again, "you reward everyone according to his conduct and as his deeds deserve" (32:19b). Here the prophet remembers that the Lord is "a jealous God, punishing the children for the sin of the fathers to the third and fourth generation of those who hate me" (Ex. 20:5). Modern pagans sometimes feel uneasy about God's justice, as if it is wrong for God to punish sin. It is not wrong; it is right! Since it is right, God is to be praised for maintaining his honor and his holiness by judging his enemies.

Next Jeremiah worships God for knowing all things. "Your eyes are open to all the ways of men" (Jer. 32:19b). Jeremiah has been reminded of God's universal knowledge, or omniscience, when cousin Hanamel showed up at his prison cell. God knew all about the visit even before it happened, as he always does.

This prayer is rich in its praise of the attributes of God. Jeremiah worships God for his omnipotence and omniscience, for his love and justice. His prayer is informed by his doctrine of God.

The same thing ought to be true of the prayers of every Christian. You must have a theology before you can have a prayer life. Knowing the character of God precedes having intimacy with him through prayer. Too many prayers are superficial in their grasp of the character of God. Instead, they ought to be saturated with the praise of his glorious attributes.

AN ANSWER FOR THE BEWILDERED

The final part of Jeremiah's prayer concerns his situation. It is worth noticing the proportions of his prayer. The prophet spends more time praising God than he does talking about his problems. John Guest says he "offered seven parts of praise to one part of puzzlement."[11]

Here is Jeremiah's puzzlement:

> *"See how the siege ramps are built up to take the city. Because*
> *of the sword, famine and plague, the city will be handed over*
> *to the Babylonians who are attacking it. What you said has*
> *happened, as you now see. And though the city will be handed*
> *over to the Babylonians, you, O Sovereign LORD, say to me,*
> *'Buy the field with silver and have the transaction witnessed.'"*
> (32:24-25)

What is the point of Jeremiah's prayer? He does not actually make a request. He does not ask God for anything. He simply tells God what God already knows; namely, that the Babylonian siege engines are at the gates and that he has just made the worst financial decision of his life.

Jeremiah's prayer sounds like a complaint. The word *though* is not in the Hebrew text, but it properly captures the reproach in Jeremiah's voice: "And you, you tell me, 'Buy the field!'" (32:25). Jeremiah calls attention to the fact that God has told him to buy the property, even though it does not take a military genius to figure out that Jerusalem is on the verge of surrender. He is perplexed by the whole thing, even flabbergasted. He does not understand what God is doing. So his prayer ends with a question mark. "You're telling me to invest in real estate, Lord? Seriously?"

Or perhaps Jeremiah does not even make it to the question mark. It sounds as if he runs out of prayer before he figures out what to pray, which is the way bewildered prayers often end.

As God responds to Jeremiah's prayer, he is not in the least bewildered: "I am the LORD, the God of all mankind. Is anything too hard for me?" (32:27). Literally, "Is anything too marvelous for me?" "Is anything too difficult, too wonderful, too extraordinary for me?"

Of course not! In fact, Jeremiah said as much at the beginning of his prayer. With his own lips he prayed, "Nothing is too hard for you" (32:17). If Jeremiah would listen to his own prayer, he could answer his own question. Nothing is too wonderful for God. If God says he will rebuild Jerusalem, then rebuild it he will. And if God says it is a good time to buy, then it is a buyer's market for men and women of faith.

Jeremiah's example shows the value of praying with an informed view of God, especially during desperate times. Approach God with a proper sense of his power, love, justice, and knowledge. Then you will find the faith to trust him, even when he tells you to fork over seventeen shekels to cousin Hanamel.

CHAPTER 12

BOOK

BURNING

It was the ninth month and the king was sitting in the winter apartment, with a fire burning in the firepot in front of him. Whenever Jehudi had read three or four columns of the scroll, the king cut them off with a scribe's knife and threw them into the firepot, until the entire scroll was burned in the fire. The king and all his attendants who heard all these words showed no fear, nor did they tear their clothes.

JEREMIAH 36:22-24

Among the many reasons to trust the Bible is its staying power. As the Puritan Thomas Watson (d. 1690) rightly observed, the enemies of God have often tried—unsuccessfully!—to extinguish the light of Scripture:

> We may know the Scripture to be the Word of God by its miraculous preservation in all ages. The holy Scriptures are the richest jewel that Christ has left us; and the church of God has so kept these public records of heaven, that they have not been lost. The Word of God has never wanted enemies to oppose, and, if possible, to extirpate it. . . . but God has preserved this blessed Book inviolable to this day. The devil and his agents have been blowing at Scripture light, but could never blow it out; a clear sign that it was lighted from heaven.[1]

Once God's enemies even tried to burn the Bible. During the days when Jehoiakim reigned in Judah, all Jeremiah's prophecies were written on a scroll and taken to the king in his winter apartment. As he sat warming himself by the fire, Jehoiakim used the Word of God for kindling.

In chapter 36, therefore, the entire book of Jeremiah hangs in the balance. If Jehoiakim succeeds, there will be no Jeremiah: no warnings about spiritual adultery (chapters 2—3); no signpost at the crossroads pointing out the ancient path (6:16); no boasting in the knowledge of God (9:24); no taunting the scarecrow in the melon patch (10:5); no visiting the potter's house (chapters 18—19); no seeking the peace and prosperity of the city (29:7); and no promise of the New Covenant (31:31-34). Everything Jeremiah ever prophesied will go up in smoke.

Yet to this day the church holds the prophecies of Jeremiah as a sacred treasure. All of them. One reason the Scripture is known to be the Word of God is because of its miraculous preservation throughout all ages.

WRITING THE WORD

Jeremiah 36 is about the writing, receiving, rejecting, and preserving of the Bible.

First, the writing: The Word of God passed from the mind of the Holy Spirit to the pages of the Bible:

> *In the fourth year of Jehoiakim son of Josiah king of Judah, this word came to Jeremiah from the LORD: "Take a scroll and write on it all the words I have spoken to you concerning Israel, Judah and all the other nations from the time I began speaking to you in the reign of Josiah till now." (36:1-2)*

This transcription took place in 605 B.C., the year the Babylonians won a momentous military victory over the Egyptians at

Carchemish. God tells Jeremiah to write down all the prophecies he has received in his first twenty years of ministry.

It is often pointed out that Jeremiah's scroll had to be short enough to be read three times in one day. This is because the events of verses 8-26 seem to have transpired in a single day. However, most scholars overestimate the amount of time such readings would take. It is reasonable to think that this scroll contained all (or nearly all) the prophecies that now comprise Jeremiah chapters 1—25 and 46—51.

The words Jeremiah wrote down were not his words; they were God's words. Although the book reflects the personality and experiences of the man Jeremiah, its ultimate author is the Holy Spirit. When the writer to the Hebrews quoted from the book of Jeremiah he wrote, "The Holy Spirit also testifies" (Heb. 10:15). Thus, what Peter wrote about biblical prophecy applies to Jeremiah: "Above all, you must understand that no prophecy of Scripture came about by the prophet's own interpretation. For prophecy never had its origin in the will of man, but men spoke from God as they were carried along by the Holy Spirit" (2 Pet. 1:20-21). In other words, the Word of God is the Word of *God*. The words in Jeremiah's book are not words about God, they are words *from* God, which is why they never lose their power.

The reason God wanted his words written down was to save his people from their sins. "Perhaps when the people of Judah hear about every disaster I plan to inflict on them, each of them will turn from his wicked way; then I will forgive their wickedness and their sin" (Jer. 36:3). This verse helps explain Jeremiah's many terrible prophecies of divine judgment. They are not intended simply to terrify; they are also intended to save. "God wants to do more than convict; he wants to convert."[2] This is a hope Jeremiah shares, for he says, "Perhaps they will bring their petition before the LORD, and each will turn from his wicked ways, for the anger and wrath pronounced against this people by the LORD are great" (36:7).

All God's threatenings have the gracious purpose of turning sinners away from their sins. As Derek Kidner asks, "Why else should he pour out threats rather than immediate actions, unless it is to bring us to our senses and to his feet?"[3] The preaching of final judgment and eternal punishment is founded upon the grace of God. The Word of God tells us we deserve to be damned, in order to make us run to Christ to be saved.

For Scripture to fulfill that saving purpose, it has to be written down. The divine words Jeremiah has committed to memory need to be put on paper. "So Jeremiah called Baruch son of Neriah, and while Jeremiah dictated all the words the LORD had spoken to him, Baruch wrote them on the scroll" (36:4). This is how many parts of the Bible were recorded. First, they were revealed; then they were remembered; then they were written down. The book of Jeremiah was revealed by the Holy Spirit, remembered by the prophet Jeremiah, and written down by the learned Baruch.

Baruch is more than a scribe; he is Jeremiah's executive secretary. In addition to taking dictation, he handles publicity:

> Jeremiah told Baruch, "I am restricted; I cannot go to the LORD's temple. So you go to the house of the LORD on a day of fasting and read to the people from the scroll the words of the LORD that you wrote as I dictated. Read them to all the people of Judah who come in from their towns." (36:5-6)

So Baruch goes to the temple. It is now nearly a year after Jeremiah has begun to work on his scroll (December, 604 B.C.). A fast has been proclaimed throughout Judah (36:9), probably because the Babylonian victory over the Philistines at Ashkelon has created a national panic. Jeremiah himself is barred from going to the temple. Either the Lord has prevented him from going, or he is ceremonially unclean, or his notorious Temple Sermon has made him Public Enemy Number One (26:1-19; cf.

7:1—8:3). In any case, Baruch is the one chosen to risk his life
for the sake of God's Word.

RECEIVING THE WORD

Baruch has some misgivings about serving as Jeremiah's "stunt
double" (see chapter 45). Nevertheless, he

> *did everything Jeremiah the prophet told him to do; at the*
> *LORD's temple he read the words of the LORD from the scroll.*
> *In the ninth month of the fifth year of Jehoiakim son of Josiah*
> *king of Judah, a time of fasting before the LORD was pro-*
> *claimed for all the people in Jerusalem and those who had come*
> *from the towns of Judah. From the room of Gemariah son of*
> *Shaphan the secretary, which was in the upper courtyard at the*
> *entrance of the New Gate of the temple, Baruch read to all the*
> *people at the LORD's temple the words of Jeremiah from the*
> *scroll.* (36:8-10)

When it is first "published," Jeremiah's book receives mixed
reviews. Baruch reads it to everyone he can, but most people are
too busy with the ritual of fasting actually to repent! (7:2 ff.). One
man, however, is hanging on Jeremiah's every prophecy. His
name is Micaiah.

Micaiah demonstrates the proper way to receive God's Word.
First comes the *hearing* of the Word: "Micaiah son of Gemariah,
the son of Shaphan, heard all the words of the LORD from the
scroll" (36:11). He listens to God's Word in its entirety. He
doesn't doze off in the middle of the reading or leave before
Baruch is finished. Micaiah listens to Jeremiah's prophecies from
beginning to end.

The members of Jehoiakim's royal cabinet also listen atten-
tively to the whole counsel of God. When Micaiah tells them
about the scroll, they are not satisfied with a book report. They
send for Baruch:

"Bring the scroll from which you have read to the people and
come." So Baruch son of Neriah went to them with the scroll in
his hand. They said to him, "Sit down, please, and read it to us."
   So Baruch read it to them. When they heard all these words.
. . . (36:14b-16a)

Like Micaiah, these officials are careful hearers of God's Word.
Receiving the Word begins with hearing it from beginning to
end. This is why expository preaching is so necessary. It takes God's
Word the way God gives it: verse by verse, chapter by chapter, book
by book. This is also why systematic Bible reading is so valuable.
One place the Bible needs to be read is in church. Since the nineteenth century, the Tenth Presbyterian Church in Philadelphia has
read continuously through the Psalms and the New Testament during its morning worship services. At the end of Psalm 150 the congregation starts all over again with Psalm 1; the last chapter of
Revelation is followed by the first chapter of Matthew.

Another place the Bible needs to be read is at home. Every
Christian needs to make a regular practice of reading the Word
of God. Get a Bible, get a bookmark, and start reading. Use the
monthly study guide produced by the Bible Study Hour, *God's
Word Today*.[4] Or get a copy of Robert Murray M'Cheyne's
Calendar for Daily Readings and read the whole Bible in a year.[5]
Receiving God's Word means hearing it, and the best way to hear
it is to take it whole.

Next comes the *fearing* of God's Word. When Micaiah hears
that God is angry against Judah's sin, he fears the Lord greatly.
Immediately he goes to tell his father and the other officials (36:11-
12). "When they heard all these words, they looked at each other
in fear" (36:16). Literally, they trembled in front of one another.
The cabinet realizes that their nation is about to be judged.

It is one thing to hear God's Word. It is another to fear it,
heeding all God's warnings, trusting all God's promises, and
obeying all God's commands. To fear God's Word is to confess

you are a sinner, trust that Jesus died on the cross for your sins, and live the rest of your life according to God's will.

Then comes *sharing* God's Word. To receive it properly means to pass it on to others. When Micaiah hears words of divine judgment, he cannot keep them to himself. "He went down to the secretary's room in the royal palace, where all the officials were sitting." There he "told them everything he had heard Baruch read to the people from the scroll" (36:13). The cabinet, in turn, wants to tell the king. They "said to Baruch, 'We must report all these words to the king'" (36:16).

First, however, they are careful to make sure the scroll is the authentic Word of God. "They asked Baruch, 'Tell us, how did you come to write all this? Did Jeremiah dictate it?' 'Yes,' Baruch replied, 'he dictated all these words to me, and I wrote them in ink on the scroll'" (36:17-18). Once they are sure the scroll is God's written Word, the officials plead with their king to receive it respectfully. "Elnathan, Delaiah and Gemariah urged the king not to burn the scroll" (36:25).

These men are passionate evangelists. They are not content to hear the Word of God for themselves; they want others to hear it as well. And they want others to hear the whole thing. Micaiah told them "everything" he had heard (36:13). The cabinet reported "all these words" to the king (36:16). This is all the more impressive when we remember that what these men are reporting so thoroughly is not good news. It is all about God's judgment against sin.

Too much contemporary evangelism fails to take the wrath of God seriously. Many Christians testify to the grace and goodness of God. Yet how often do they explain how much God hates sin and how severely he intends to deal with it? News of divine judgment has an essential place in evangelism. People have to hear the bad news about sin and death before they can receive the good news about forgiveness and new life in Christ.

Receiving God's Word means hearing it fully, fearing it greatly, and sharing it unstintingly. It is no surprise that Micaiah received the Word of God this way. After all, he was a grandson of Shaphan. Shaphan was the great man who served as Secretary of State under King Josiah. When the Book of Law was rediscovered in the temple, Shaphan read it and reread it for the king (2 Kings 22; cf. 2 Chron. 34).

Shaphan was also a good father. Great spiritual leaders do not always raise godly children. Often they do not. But Shaphan was a good father as well as a great leader. His sons were among the forgotten heroes of the Bible. "Ahikam son of Shaphan supported Jeremiah, and so he was not handed over to the people to be put to death" (Jer. 26:24). Elasah son of Shaphan carried Jeremiah's letter to the exiles in Babylon (29:3). Gemariah son of Shaphan was one of the officials who took Jeremiah's scroll to Jehoiakim (36:12, 20).[6]

The godly influence of Shaphan extended to his grandchildren. Micaiah son of Gemariah, the son of Shaphan, shared God's Word with the king's cabinet (36:11-14). His cousin Gedaliah, son of Ahikam, the son of Shaphan, rescued Jeremiah and brought him into his own home when Jerusalem fell (39:14; cf. chapters 40—41). Eventually Gedaliah became governor of the Jewish remnant in Jerusalem (40:7).

The sons and grandsons of Shaphan were great men of God. They were national leaders and lovers of God's Word. Therefore, Shaphan is a model for Christian parents living in a pagan culture. Fathers like Shaphan raise sons and daughters who will go anywhere and do anything to share God's Word.

REJECTING THE WORD

Jehoiakim does exactly the opposite. He will not hear God's Word and does not fear it. In fact, he tries to make sure it will never be shared again. His private book burning shows the awful consequences of rejecting God's Word.

Jehoiakim has never been a godly king. His cabinet members rarely know how he will react, so they are always prepared for the worst. This time they take the precaution of hiding the scroll and sending Baruch and Jeremiah underground:

> Then the officials said to Baruch, "You and Jeremiah, go and hide. Don't let anyone know where you are."
> After they put the scroll in the room of Elishama the secretary, they went to the king in the courtyard and reported everything to him. (36:19-20)

These are necessary precautions. After all, Jehoiakim has been so angry with the prophet Uriah that he has had him extradited from Egypt and executed (26:22-33).

The scene for the third reading of Baruch's scroll is among the most memorable in the Bible:

> The king sent Jehudi to get the scroll, and Jehudi brought it from the room of Elishama the secretary and read it to the king and all the officials standing beside him. It was the ninth month and the king was sitting in the winter apartment, with a fire burning in the firepot in front of him. Whenever Jehudi had read three or four columns of the scroll, the king cut them off with a scribe's knife and threw them into the firepot, until the entire scroll was burned in the fire. (36:21-23)

Jehoiakim does not even wait for Jehudi to finish. As soon as Jehudi unrolls each section of the scroll, which is written on leather or papyrus and wrapped around wooden rollers, the king carries out his outrageous act of censorship. He methodically uses a scribe's penknife to cut and burn holy Scripture.

Perhaps Jehoiakim doubts the reality of divine judgment. He later asks Jeremiah, "Why did you write on it that the king of

Babylon would certainly come and destroy this land and cut off both men and animals from it?" (36:29).

Or perhaps Jehoiakim thinks burning God's Word will prevent his doom from coming to pass. If so, he fails to recognize that the power of the Word flows from the power of God himself. J. I. Packer once commented, "Jehoiakim burns God's Word, ignoring its warnings. That's like getting out of a car to destroy a 'Bridge Out' sign: done at one's own peril."[7]

The shocking thing is not so much Jehoiakim's stupidity as his audacity. Jehoiakim is casual, almost nonchalant in his defiance of God's Word. "The king and all his attendants who heard all these words showed no fear, nor did they tear their clothes" (36:24). The arrogance, the contempt, the insolence of the man! He turns a deaf ear to the counselors who plead with him not to do this wicked thing (36:25). Then he adds injury to insult by calling for the arrest of Baruch and Jeremiah (36:26).

It was a very different scene when the Book of the Law was discovered in the days of King Josiah. When that good king heard God's words, he did not tear the words, but his clothes, as a sign of repentance (2 Kings 22:11). These are the only two ways to respond to God's Word: either to receive it or to reject it. Either to hear it or to ignore it. Either to fear it or to forget it. Dwight L. Moody once described the difference between men like Josiah and men like Jehoiakim this way: "Either the Bible will keep you from sin, or sin will keep you from the Bible."

There are many sons and daughters of Jehoiakim in the world today. Sinners who will not sit still long enough to hear a biblical sermon. Bible scholars who cut and paste the Bible rather than receiving it as the Word of God. Churchgoers who only open their Bibles in the pews on Sunday. Ministers who spend all their time thinking about how a passage will preach and never figure out how it applies to the preacher.

Most evangelicals consider themselves to be students of the Word of God. Maybe we are. But could it be that we are more like Jehoiakim than Micaiah? Could it be that we spend as much time avoiding the implications of God's Word as we do studying it? J. I. Packer gives this wise warning: "The privilege of knowing God's truth with certainty and precision carries with it the responsibility of obeying that truth with equal precision."[8]

PRESERVING THE WORD

With so many enemies of God's Word in the world, it is a wonder there is any Bible left to read. Yet the Word of God is indestructible. No sooner had the first edition of Jeremiah been reduced to ashes than the second went into production:

> *After the king burned the scroll containing the words that Baruch had written at Jeremiah's dictation, the word of the LORD came to Jeremiah: "Take another scroll and write on it all the words that were on the first scroll, which Jehoiakim king of Judah burned up."* . . . *So Jeremiah took another scroll and gave it to the scribe Baruch son of Neriah, and as Jeremiah dictated, Baruch wrote on it all the words of the scroll that Jehoiakim king of Judah had burned in the fire. And many similar words were added to them.* (Jer. 36:27-28, 32)

Notice that *all* the words from the first scroll are recorded on the second. Even if Jeremiah has forgotten what he prophesied, the Spirit remembers.

One of the great ironies of the Bible is that Jehoiakim himself makes an appearance in the expanded edition of Jeremiah's manuscript. For among the "many similar words" added are some that pertain specifically to the king:

> *"Therefore, this is what the LORD says about Jehoiakim king of Judah: He will have no one to sit on the throne of David; his body will be thrown out and exposed to the heat by day and the frost by night. I will punish him and his children and his attendants for their wickedness; I will bring on them and those*

living in Jerusalem and the people of Judah every disaster I pro-
nounced against them, because they have not listened." (36:30-
31; cf. 22:13-19)

Jeremiah's mention of the throne of David does not mean
that the Davidic line had come to an end. It means that
Jehoiakim's offspring would not rule in Jerusalem for long.
Jehoiakim's son Jehoiachin would reign for only three months,
and his uncle rather than his son succeeded him (2 Kings 24).

For Jehoiakim himself there is another irony: The king who
burned the Bible because he was so anxious to keep warm will
be "exposed to the heat by day and the frost by night" (Jer.
36:30). His children, his attendants, and the whole nation will
also be judged, and for this reason: "because they have not listened" (36:31b). God holds people responsible for what they do
not do as well as for what they do.

God always has the last word. His words outlast their enemies. The endurance of the Bible attests to the remarkable, at times
miraculous, preservation of the Word of God. Satan has done his
worst to prevent the production, translation, and proclamation of
God's Word. But he has completely and utterly failed.

Consider all the reliable manuscripts of the Bible. The books
of the Bible are far and away the best-attested writings of the
ancient world. Think of the great number of accurate translations
now available in English. Or the work of Bible translation going
on this very moment all over the globe. Sometime in the twenty-
first century the Gospels of Jesus Christ will be available in every
known language. Some time after that the prophecies of
Jeremiah—the very words Jehoiakim cut from the scroll and
burned in his firepot—will be read around the world by every
tribe and people and nation.

The Word of God may be despised, but it will never be
destroyed. The *Westminster Confession of Faith* remarks: "The
Old Testament in Hebrew and the New Testament in Greek,

being immediately inspired by God, by His singular care and providence" have been "kept pure in all ages."⁹

There are many remarkable stories of the preservation of the Bible. One of the best comes from the early days of the English Reformation, when William Tyndale (c. 1494-1536) had just published the first translation of the New Testament in the English language (1528).

In his great rage against the Protestant Gospel, Archbishop Wolsey began to burn copies of Tyndale's Testament at St. Paul's Cathedral in London. The Catholics needed a steady supply of Bibles to burn, so the bishop of London tried to buy as many as possible in Antwerp, where the Bibles were printed.

The historical account of the bishop's errand deserves to be repeated in full:

> And so it happened that one Augustine Packington, a mercer and merchant of London, and of a great honesty, the same time was in Antwerp, where the bishop then was, and this Packington was a man that highly favoured William Tyndale, but to the bishop utterly showed himself to the contrary. The bishop desirous to have his purpose brought to pass, communed of the New Testaments, and how gladly he would buy them.
>
> Packington then hearing what he wished for, said unto the bishop. My Lord if it be your pleasure, I can in this matter do more I dare say, than most of the merchants of England that are here, for I know the Dutch men and strangers that have brought them of Tyndale, and have them here to sell, so that if it be your lordship's pleasure, to pay for them, I will then assure you, to have every book of them, that is imprinted and is here unsold.
>
> The bishop thinking that he had God by the toe, when indeed he had (as after he thought) the Devil by the fist, said, gentle Master Packington, do your diligence and get them and with all my heart I will pay for them, whatsoever they cost you, for the books are erroneous and naughts and I

intend surely to destroy them all, and to burn them at Paul's Cross.

Augustine Packington came to William Tyndale and said, William I know thou art a poor man, and hast a heap of New Testaments, and books by thee, for the which thou hast both endangered thy friends, and beggared thyself, and I have now gotten thee a merchant, which with ready money shall dispatch thee of all that thou hast, if you think it so profitable for yourself.

Who is the merchant said Tyndale?

The bishop of London said Packington.

O that is because he will burn them said Tyndale, yea marry quoth Packington. I am the gladder said Tyndale, for these two benefits shall come thereon, I shall get money of him for these books, to bring myself out of debt, (and the whole world shall cry out upon the burning of God's word). And the overplus of the money, that shall remain to me, shall make me more studious, to correct the said New Testament, and so newly to imprint the same once again, and I trust the second will much better like you, than ever did the first: And so forward went the bargain, the bishop had the books, Packington had the thanks, and Tyndale had the money.

Afterward, when more New Testaments were printed, they came thick and threefold into England, the bishop of London hearing that still there were so many New Testaments abroad, sent for Augustine Packington and said unto him: Sir how cometh this, that there are so many New Testaments abroad, and you promised and assured me, that you had bought all?[10]

Had the bishop bothered to look, he could have found his answer in the pages of Tyndale's New Testament: "The grass withereth, and the flower falleth away: But the word of the Lord endureth ever" (1 Pet. 1:24b-25a).

CHAPTER 13

Brands from
the Burning

*"Go and tell Ebed-Melech the Cushite, 'This is what the
LORD Almighty, the God of Israel, says: I am about to fulfill
my words against this city through disaster, not prosperity. At
that time they will be fulfilled before your eyes. But I will rescue you on that day, declares the LORD; you will not be
handed over to those you fear. I will save you; you will not
fall by the sword but will escape with your life, because you
trust in me, declares the LORD.'"*

JEREMIAH 39:16-18

Try to picture this scene:

> *Because of thirst the infant's tongue*
>   *sticks to the roof of its mouth;*
> *the children beg for bread,*
>   *but no one gives it to them.*
> *Those who once ate delicacies*
>   *are destitute in the streets.*
> *Those nurtured in purple*
>   *now lie on ash heaps. . . .*
> *Those killed by the sword are better off*
>   *than those who die of famine;*
> *racked with hunger, they waste away*
>   *for lack of food from the field.*
> *With their own hands compassionate women*
>   *have cooked their own children,*

> *who became their food*
> *when my people were destroyed.*
> *The LORD has given full vent to his wrath;*
> *he has poured out his fierce anger.*
> *He kindled a fire in Zion*
> *that consumed her foundations. . . .*
> *Men stalked us at every step,*
> *so we could not walk in our streets.*
> *Our end was near, our days were numbered,*
> *for our end had come.* (Lam. 4:4-5, 9-11, 18)

These lines were written by the prophet Jeremiah. They form an eyewitness account of the last, desperate days leading up to the fall of Jerusalem. After eighteen long months of siege, the Babylonian army marched into Jerusalem for the last time in July of 587 B.C.

According to Josephus, the historian (A.D. 37-c. 100):

> The battering ram took its last run at the walls. Darts from the enemy siege mounds arched into the midnight sky and struck their mark in flames. Famine had already claimed many lives inside the walls. Five Babylonian princes marched through the streets of Jerusalem, their faces illuminated by the flames of destruction.[1]

These historical reports have been confirmed by the archaeologist Katherine Kenyon, who has shown how the walls and houses of Jerusalem were reduced to rubble.[2] The fall of Jerusalem was an epochal event in world history. The city did not return to Jewish rule until the middle of the twentieth century, some 2,500 years later.

JERUSALEM BURNING

The fall of Jerusalem was also an important event in redemptive history. It proved that all God's promises of judgment come true.

Jeremiah's report of the day of judgment is restrained. He

gives a sober account of Jerusalem's fall, explaining who occupied the city, when, and how:

> *This is how Jerusalem was taken: In the ninth year of*
> *Zedekiah king of Judah, in the tenth month, Nebuchadnezzar*
> *king of Babylon marched against Jerusalem with his whole*
> *army and laid siege to it. And on the ninth day of the fourth*
> *month of Zedekiah's eleventh year, the city wall was broken*
> *through. Then all the officials of the king of Babylon came*
> *and took seats in the Middle Gate: Nergal-Sharezer of Samgar,*
> *Nebo-Sarsekim a chief officer, Nergal-Sharezer a high official*
> *and the other officials of the king of Babylon.*
> (Jer. 39:1-3; cf. 2 Kings 25:1-4)

This is how ancient generals claimed victory over a defeated
city. The victors would take their seats in the city gates. In triumph they would claim the place of rule and governance.
Jeremiah lists some Babylonian names to show that Judah's con-
querors speak a strange and unfamiliar tongue (cf. 5:15).

Once they took the city, "the Babylonians set fire to the royal
palace and the houses of the people and broke down the walls of
Jerusalem" (39:8; cf. 2 Kings 25:8-10). Palaces, houses, walls—
everything was torched. Then the best and brightest of the Jews
were deported to Babylon. "Nebuzaradan commander of the
imperial guard carried into exile to Babylon the people who
remained in the city, along with those who had gone over to him,
and the rest of the people" (Jer. 39:9).

These verses form the climax of Jeremiah's book . . . and the
low point of Jeremiah's life. From the first verse of the first chapter, his prophecies have marched relentlessly toward the day of
Jerusalem's destruction. Although in this passage he writes with
the detachment of a historian, every word strikes like a hammer.
The dreaded day has finally come.

On the day of judgment every promise God ever made about
the fall of Jerusalem comes true (cf. 2 Kings 25:1-26; Jer. 52:4-

30). God said disaster would come from the north (1:14; 4:6; 6:22; 13:20), and disaster comes from the north. God said a strange foreign nation would attack (5:15), and a strange foreign nation has attacked. God said Jerusalem would be surrounded and besieged (4:17; 6:3, 6; cf. Ezek. 4:1-3), and Jerusalem is now surrounded and besieged. God said there would be famine in the land (14:1-6, 16, 18; 18:21; cf. Ezek. 4:16-17), and there is famine in the land. God said the whole land would be laid waste (25:11), and the whole land is laid waste. God said nations and kingdoms would be torn down (1:10; cf. 39:8), and the nation of Judah is torn down, stone by stone.

The list of fulfilled prophecies goes on and on. God said death would enter the city (9:21; cf. 15:7-9; 18:21), and death enters the city. God said kings would "come and set up their thrones in the entrance of the gates of Jerusalem" (1:15). The kings have come, they have conquered, and they have taken their seats. God promised that the city would be burned (21:10, 14; 32:29; 34:2, 22; 37:8; 38:18, 23; cf. Ezek. 5:1-4), and the city is reduced to ashes. God said his people would be taken into exile (10:17-18; 13:17-19; 15:14; 17:4), and they are taken into exile.

God even promised, through the prophet Ezekiel, "I will bring him [Zedekiah] to Babylonia, the land of the Chaldeans, but he will not see it, and there he will die" (Ezek. 12:13). This curious prophecy is fulfilled when Zedekiah is blinded before his arrival in Babylon; he will go to that great city but he will never see it!

The fall of Jerusalem confirmed many specific promises of divine judgment. All Jeremiah's prophecies of destruction came true. Calvin thus refers to chapter 39 as "the proof of all his former doctrine."[3] Twice God told Jeremiah, "Listen! I am going to bring on Judah and on everyone living in Jerusalem every disaster I pronounced against them" (Jer. 35:17a; cf. 19:15). He meant what he said. God delivered *every* disaster God promised.

Lest there be any doubt about who has brought these things to pass, he says, "*I* am about to fulfill my words against this city through disaster" (39:16).

THE JUDGMENT TO COME

Many of Jeremiah's contemporaries doubted the day of judgment would ever come. The religious leaders were promising "peace, peace," rather than the sword (6:14; 8:11). By and large, the people of Jerusalem did not believe in the wrath of God, despite many warnings to the contrary.

The same is true in these pagan times. The person on the street lives in ignorance of Christ's imminent return. The final judgment is generally treated as a humorous subject. The man carrying the sign that reads, "Repent—The End Is Near" is either mocked or ignored. The place hell is most likely to be mentioned in American culture is on the comics page in the newspaper. Doubts about the reality of judgment and eternal damnation have also entered the church. As John Blanchard has asked, *Whatever Happened to Hell?*[4]

The apostle Peter promised this would happen. "You must understand that in the last days scoffers will come, scoffing and following their own evil desires. They will say, 'Where is this "coming" he promised? Ever since our fathers died, everything goes on as it has since the beginning of creation'" (2 Pet. 3:3-4). Peter was right. The people of this generation do not believe in the wrath of God, do not look for the coming of Christ, and do not fear the day of judgment.

Therefore, the question must be asked and answered: What does the Bible say will happen on the day of judgment?

First, the Lord Jesus Christ will return. He will return personally. As the angel said to the disciples, "This same Jesus, who has been taken from you into heaven, will come back in the same way you have seen him go into heaven" (Acts 1:11). He will return impressively. "The Lord himself will come down from heaven, with a loud command, with the voice of the archangel and with the trumpet call of God" (1 Thess. 4:16). And he will return visibly: "Look, he is coming with the clouds, and every eye will see him" (Rev. 1:7a).

The personal, impressive, visible return of Jesus Christ will be sudden and cataclysmic:

> The present heavens and earth are reserved for fire, being kept for the day of judgment and destruction of ungodly men. . . . But the day of the Lord will come like a thief. The heavens will disappear with a roar; the elements will be destroyed by fire, and the earth and everything in it will be laid bare. . . . That day will bring about the destruction of the heavens by fire, and the elements will melt in the heat. (2 Pet. 3:7, 10, 12)

No one knows when the day of judgment will come (cf. Matt. 24:36). But when it does come, everything in the heavens and the earth will be destroyed. The conflagration in Jerusalem was a warning of what will happen to the entire cosmos at the end of history. The whole universe—with all its stars, planets, comets, and galaxies—will undergo instantaneous heat death.

Furthermore, the Bible says it will be a day of reckoning. God "has set a day when he will judge the world with justice by the man he has appointed" (Acts 17:31). The dead will be raised, and every man, woman, and child who has ever lived will be gathered before the throne of God for judgment. Then God "will give to each person according to what he has done" (Rom. 2:6). "For we must all appear before the judgment seat of Christ" (2 Cor. 5:10; cf. John 5:25-29). As Jesus himself has promised, "When the Son of Man comes in his glory, and all the angels with him, he will sit on his throne in heavenly glory. All the nations will be gathered before him, and he will separate the people one from another as a shepherd separates the sheep from the goats" (Matt. 25:31-32).

"DEPART FROM ME, YOU WHO ARE CURSED"

There is a second question to be asked about the day of judgment. The first has already been asked and answered from Scripture: What will happen on the day of judgment? The second must be answered within every human heart: What will happen to *me* on the day of judgment?

Not everyone will meet the same end. There will be two different kinds of people on that day: the sheep and the goats; the righteous and the unrighteous. These two peoples will have two very different destinies. Some will be saved, while the rest will be lost forever. Some will walk through pearly gates into the heavenly city of gold (Rev. 21:21), while the rest will be condemned to an eternal hell of fire (Matt. 18:9; cf. Rev. 20:11-15). Jesus promises that the unrighteous "will go away to eternal punishment, but the righteous to eternal life" (Matt. 25:46).

The burning of Jerusalem is a picture of the final judgment. There were also two kinds of people on that day: the righteous and the unrighteous. And they met two very different ends. Some were saved and some were lost. Some were redeemed and some were damned.

Zedekiah was lost. Zedekiah was the king who could never make up his mind whether he wanted to follow God or not. So when the day of judgment comes, there is no one to save him but himself. The Bible gives a glimpse of his desperate attempt to escape by a secret route to the valley. "When Zedekiah king of Judah and all the soldiers saw them [the Babylonian generals], they fled; they left the city at night by way of the king's garden, through the gate between the two walls, and headed toward the Arabah" (Jer. 39:4; cf. Ezek. 12:12). Zedekiah abandons ship like a coward instead of going down with it like a worthy captain.

Zedekiah does not get very far, however. The fugitives can run, but they can't hide. "The Babylonian army pursued them and overtook Zedekiah in the plains of Jericho" (39:5a). The soldiers capture them and bring them to Nebuchadnezzar's field headquarters, where Zedekiah receives summary military justice:

> *They captured him and took him to Nebuchadnezzar king of Babylon at Riblah in the land of Hamath, where he pronounced sentence on him. There at Riblah the king of Babylon slaughtered the sons of Zedekiah before his eyes and also killed all the nobles of Judah. Then he put out Zedekiah's eyes and bound him with bronze shackles to take him to Babylon. (39:5-7)*

Zedekiah receives the punishment God has long promised for his sins. And worse. Jeremiah has prophesied that the king of Judah will not escape (38:18), but will see the king of Babylon with his own eyes (34:3). What he has not prophesied is that Zedekiah will see his sons, the princes of Judah, butchered before his very eyes. Or that Nebuchadnezzar will blind him as well as bind him. In an act of cruel barbarity, Nebuchadnezzar tears out Zedekiah's eyes. In the words of one commentator: "The brutal death of his sons is the last thing he sees, the last thing he will ever see, the thing he will see as long as he lives."[5]

Zedekiah's fate finds an echo in the torture of Gloucester in William Shakespeare's *King Lear*. Taking knife to eyeball, his wicked daughter Cornwall says, "Out, vile jelly!" to which Gloucester responds, "All dark and comfortless."[6] For Zedekiah, as for Gloucester, all is dark and comfortless. How he must now long for death on his long, slow, dark march to Babylon. The day of judgment has turned out to be far worse than he ever could have imagined.

Like Zedekiah, many people hope to escape the day of judgment. They doubt the personal return of Jesus Christ to judge the world. They hope that the wrath of God has been exaggerated. They deny the existence of hell. They think they are good enough to get to heaven. They expect to have time to slip out the garden door and run for dear life.

Jeremiah 39 stands as a warning against every naïve hope of escaping the judgment to come. Zedekiah suffered a fate worse than death. To his dismay, he discovered the day of judgment to be a living hell.

The saddest thing about the final chapter in Zedekiah's tragic story is that the king could have written a happy ending. Right up until the very end, God gives him every opportunity to repent for his sins (38:20). Repeatedly Jeremiah comes to Zedekiah and pleads with him to turn to God in faith and repentance. But the king rejects every last entreaty.

If the Holy Spirit has warned you of divine judgment, do not be so foolish. At this very moment God is giving you the same chance he gave Zedekiah. It is the chance—perhaps your last—to confess your sins, believe in Jesus Christ, and escape the judgment to come.

"COME, YOU WHO ARE BLESSED BY MY FATHER"

Happily, not everyone will be lost on the day of judgment. Although the fall of Jerusalem is a day of damnation for some, it is a day of salvation for others. The poor are made rich and slaves receive their freedom: "Nebuzaradan the commander of the guard left behind in the land of Judah some of the poor people, who owned nothing; and at that time he gave them vineyards and fields" (39:10).

It is also a day of salvation for God's servants. As the city burns, Jeremiah and Ebed-Melech are delivered from death like brands snatched from the burning.

Jeremiah is saved from judgment because—somewhat unexpectedly—he has friends in high places. "Now Nebuchadnezzar king of Babylon had given these orders about Jeremiah through Nebuzaradan commander of the imperial guard: 'Take him and look after him; don't harm him but do for him whatever he asks'" (39:11-12). Even in the chaos of the fallen city, Jeremiah is not forgotten. Why Nebuchadnezzar takes notice of him is a mystery. Perhaps he has respect for prophets (cf. Dan. 4:34-37). Perhaps some of the Jews who deserted to the Babylonians have told him about the man who has begged the city to surrender. In any case, by the providence of God Jeremiah's life is spared.

God will not forget his friends on the day of judgment. It is easy to be overlooked in this world. Every day people get left behind by the bus. Birthdays are ignored and anniversaries are forgotten. Applications get misplaced and packages get lost in the mail. But God will not leave behind, ignore, forget, misplace, or lose a single believer on the day of judgment. Like Jeremiah, every child of God will be saved.

The contrast between Zedekiah and Jeremiah illustrates the teaching of Jesus Christ: "Whoever wants to save his life will lose it, but whoever loses his life for me will save it" (Luke 9:24). The king did everything he could to save his life and lost it. Jeremiah threw away his life for God and saved it.

God not only saves Jeremiah's life, but he also gives him a royal escort: "Nebuzaradan the commander of the guard, Nebushazban a chief officer, Nergal-Sharezer a high official and all the other officers of the king of Babylon sent and had Jeremiah taken out of the courtyard of the guard" (Jer. 39:13). Then Jeremiah is received into the care of godly friends: "They turned him over to Gedaliah son of Ahikam, the son of Shaphan, to take him back to his home. So Jeremiah remained among his own people" (39:14).

Gedaliah, as we have seen, is a good man. He is a member of the one of the godliest families left in Jerusalem. He is the grandson of Shaphan, who brought the Book of the Law to King Josiah (2 Kings 22:3-20). And he is the son of Ahikam, who defended Jeremiah's life when he was accused of blasphemy (Jer. 26:24). God has used Jeremiah's friends to save his life.

One does not have to be a famous prophet to be saved, however. Jeremiah 39 also documents the salvation of a slave:

While Jeremiah had been confined in the courtyard of the guard, the word of the LORD came to him: "Go and tell Ebed-Melech the Cushite, 'This is what the LORD Almighty, the God of Israel, says: I am about to fulfill my words against this city through disaster, not prosperity. At that time they will be fulfilled before your eyes. But I will rescue you on that day, declares the LORD; you will not be handed over to those you fear. I will save you; you will not fall by the sword but will escape with your life, because you trust in me, declares the LORD.'" (39:15-18)

These words explain what happens to Ebed-Melech on the day of Jerusalem's judgment. God has given him a quintuple guarantee of salvation: "I will rescue you; you will not be handed over; I will save you; you will not fall; you will escape with your life." The word for life (*shalal*) is actually the word for booty, or plunder taken in combat. Ebed-Melech holds on to his life like a battle prize.

Not even Ebed-Melech's enemies are able to lay a finger on him. This perhaps refers to the officials he defied when he rescued Jeremiah from the mud (38:7-13). When Ebed-Melech heard that Zedekiah had thrown Jeremiah into a cistern to die, he went to the king to plead for his life (38:9). With the king's permission he pulled the prophet to safety. He was so thoughtful he even took rags along to pad the ropes. Ebed-Melech saved Jeremiah's life.

Now, when his own life is in danger, God saves Ebed-Melech. This is a hint from the Old Testament that God offers salvation in Jesus Christ to all the nations of the world. Ebed-Melech was a Cushite from Ethiopia or the Nubian Empire. Thus, he is one of the notable North Africans of the Bible. Like the Ethiopian eunuch whom Philip baptized (Acts 8:26-40), Ebed-Melech shows that the Gospel is for every tribe and people and nation. It is for black and brown and red and white.

The basis for Ebed-Melech's salvation is important. He was not saved because God owed him a favor. He was not even saved because he had rescued Jeremiah from the cistern. If ever a man could have been saved by works, it would have been Ebed-Melech. His rescue operation demonstrated hatred of injustice and love for the ministry of God's Word. But when God promised to rescue him, the Lord did not say one word about that courageous act.

Ebed-Melech was not saved on the basis of any good work: He was saved by grace through faith. "I will save you . . . because you trust in me" (39:18). "Ebed-Melech's trust in the Lord saved him from the fate of the rest of the city. God did not commend Ebed-Melech for his compassion or courage, but only for his trust in God."[7] This African slave was saved by grace, through faith—and this not from himself, it was the gift of God—not by works (cf. Eph. 2:8-9).

This is one place where the Old Testament teaches the doctrine of justification by faith alone, a doctrine more fully explained in the New Testament. Even someone who has performed as many good works as Mother Theresa of Calcutta (1910-1997), the "saint of the gutters," cannot be declared righteous before God on the basis of personal merit. The believer does not stand before God on the basis of his or her own imperfect righteousness. Rather, the believer stands before God covered with the perfect righteousness of Jesus Christ, received by faith alone.

SNATCHED FROM THE FLAMES

The fall of Jerusalem gives a vivid picture of salvation from the judgment to come. Jeremiah and Ebed-Melech were two brands plucked from the burning city.

In the same way, every sinner who comes to Christ in faith is like a branch snatched from the flames. This image is repeated throughout the Old Testament prophets. Amos said to Israel, "You were like a burning stick snatched from the fire" (Amos

4:11). The angel of the Lord described Joshua the high priest as "a burning stick snatched from the fire" (Zech. 3:2b). Every believer is a brand from the burning.

If every believer is a brand from the burning, then two things follow. First, every Christian can join Charles Wesley (1707-1788) in praising God for a miraculous rescue:

> *Where shall my wondering soul begin?*
> *How shall I all to heaven aspire?*
> *A slave redeemed from death and sin,*
> *A brand plucked from eternal fire,*
> *How shall I equal triumphs raise,*
> *Or sing my great Deliverer's praise.*[8]

Second, saving other people from the flames is the responsibility of every Christian. There is too little urgency in the church for the salvation of the lost. What would the church be like if Christians understood that this pagan culture is about to be set aflame by the wrath of God? What would our witness be like if we saw the spiritual condition of unsaved family and friends as it actually is? And what if we accepted personal responsibility to help snatch them from the fire?

The book of Jude teaches Christians to think of themselves as spiritual firemen. "Be merciful to those who doubt; snatch others from the fire and save them; to others show mercy, mixed with fear" (Jude 22-23a). A whole course on Christian apologetics could be developed from these verses. But notice especially Jude's urgency: "Snatch others from the fire and save them."

This is perhaps the best short description of evangelistic work in the Bible. It describes the work of missions, preaching, and personal evangelism: "Snatch others from the fire and save them." Being snatched from the fire is exactly what happened to Jeremiah and Ebed-Melech when Jerusalem fell. By God's grace it is what will happen to every believer on the day of judgment.

The day of judgment will certainly come. On that dread day every soul who has ever lived will be gathered before the judgment seat of Christ. The same division will be made then that was made on the day Jerusalem fell. There will be only two kinds of people: the Jeremiahs and the Zedekiahs; the righteous and the unrighteous; the elect and the reprobate; the sheep and the goats; the redeemed and the damned.

On that day the enemies of God will be lost forever. They will be cast into the flames of hell, to the praise of the glory of God's justice. But like brands from the burning, believers in the Lord Jesus Christ will be saved. They will escape final judgment and enter eternal life. Everyone who understands these things will be sure to come to Christ in faith and repentance, and to help as many others as possible come to Christ with them.

The great Scotsman Thomas Boston once preached a long series of sermons on the final judgment. He closed with these words:

> And now, if you would be saved from the wrath to come, and never go into this place of torment, take no rest in your natural state; believe the sinfulness and misery of it, and labour to get out of it quickly, fleeing unto Jesus Christ by faith. Sin in you is the seed of hell: and, if the guilt and reigning power of it be not removed in time, they will bring you to the second death in eternity. There is no other way to get them removed, but by receiving Christ, as he is offered in the gospel, for justification and sanctification: and he is now offered to you with all his salvation. . . . And the terrors of hell, as well as the joys of heaven, are set before you, to stir you up to a cordial receiving of him, with all his salvation; and to incline you unto the way of faith and holiness, in which alone you can escape the everlasting fire. May the Lord himself make them effectual to that end![9]

Anyone who heeds this warning will be saved, like a brand from the burning.

DISCUSSION QUESTIONS

GOD FILES FOR DIVORCE

1. According to the author, when does spiritual adultery begin?
2. Think about your marriage or a marriage you respect. What does a lover do to keep love fresh? Could any of these same practices be applied to your love relationship with your Creator?
3. How would you define an idol in today's culture?
4. What drives your life, motivates you, and occupies your thoughts most? Your relationship with God or personal concerns?

A GOOD MAN IS HARD TO FIND

1. Why do you think God offers to spare Jerusalem if Jeremiah can find one righteous person? Is this a "bad deal" for the Almighty?
2. Do you "commit perjury" when you worship? How can you be more real at eleven o'clock on Sunday mornings?
3. Jeremiah's search for one righteous person illustrates the truth of what essential biblical doctrine? Explain this doctrine.
4. God's plan to redeem you from sin depends on the existence of one righteous, perfect Person. Explain how his plan works.
5. Have you received the gift of Christ's righteousness and salvation? If not, why not? If so, how did you receive it?

AT THE CROSSROADS

1. Why is Scripture just as reliable a guide for people in the twentieth century as it was for people in the first century?

2. What can you as a Christian learn from the history of the church?

3. Why is novelty often the enemy of orthodoxy?

4. How can a church that refuses to follow popular religious fads still have an approach relevant to contemporary pagans?

WHAT THE CHURCH NEEDS NOW IS REFORMATION!

1. What signs show that the evangelical church needs reformation?

2. Some people wrongly trust in the trappings of religion for salvation, but can trust in outward religious observances also be a problem for believers? Explain.

3. Why did God's people in Jeremiah's day think that their worship in the temple made them immune to God's judgment for their sin?

4. How do the following modern attitudes presume upon God's grace?

   • "I've always been this way. God understands."

   • "I don't always measure up, but nobody's perfect."

   • "It doesn't hurt anyone else."

   • "I can always repent for this later."

SOMETHING TO BOAST ABOUT

1. Why did Jeremiah summon the wailing women?

2. What is a chief duty of a Christian citizen when a nation or the church is sliding away from God? How can you do this duty?

3. What are some of the things that prompt people to boast?

4. Why is such boasting foolish?

5. Of what does the Christian have a right to boast?

THE SCARECROW IN THE MELON PATCH

1. Why was idol worship so attractive to Israel in Jeremiah's day?

2. What is the appeal of exotic religions to modern Americans? Why do evangelical Christians sometimes join these groups?

3. The author lists some modern idols. Have you ever had any of these (or similar) idols? Why? What need were you trying to meet?

4. Do you currently have any idols? Ask yourself the questions on p. 90.

5. This chapter gives many reasons why God is far better than any idols in our hearts. Name some reasons. These truths need to be more than facts in your mind. Ask God to embed them in your deepest heart.

IN THE POTTER'S HANDS

1. How does a potter working with clay illustrate God's sovereignty?

2. If the sovereignty of God causes you fear, what is the best way to respond to that fear?

3. In what ways does the sovereignty of God comfort you?

4. Have you resolved the issue of who is in control in your life? If you have not yet yielded control to God, do so now and save yourself a lot of heartache.

DARK NIGHT OF THE SOUL

1. What four lessons does Jeremiah learn about suffering?

2. Considering John 16:33, why are we surprised when trouble comes?

3. What is the best way to respond to suffering? If you have tried this response, describe what happened. If you haven't tried it, resolve to do so the next time trials come upon you.

4. Jeremiah 20 seems to show the prophet on an emotional roller coaster. Do you ever have this problem? Make a list of truths from Scripture and from your own experience of God's faithfulness in the past. File this where you can retrieve it during your next "down" time.

THE BEST-MADE PLANS

1. How does the tone and content of Jeremiah's message change during the Babylonian captivity?

2. What mission does God give the exiles?

3. Why is a challenge of this type especially pertinent to the church today?

4. Write a model prayer for your own town or city. If you wish, incorporate some of the ideas in Psalm 122. Make your prayer specific enough to cover the needs where you live.

THE NEW COVENANT

1. What is a biblical covenant?

2. What was the problem with the Old Covenant? Why was failure to keep it so serious?

3. God made seven promises when he gave the New Covenant. What were they?

4. Why is the New Covenant better than the Old? What aspect of the New Covenant means the most to you?

5. Between what two parties is the New Covenant made? Why?

BUYER'S MARKET

1. Why is there a buyer's market in real estate in the Jerusalem area?

2. What promises of God are you acting on today even though you may not see their fulfillment in your lifetime?

3. Are there some parts of Jeremiah's prayer (32:17-25) that you need to incorporate into your own prayer life? The next time you pray, try adding the missing ingredient(s).

BOOK BURNING

1. How did Jeremiah's writing procedure differ from the way most authors write their books?

2. What was the purpose for including prophecies of divine judgment?

3. How do Josiah and Jehoiakim illustrate two basic responses to the Bible? How do you respond when God speaks to you through His Word?

4. Is it possible to destroy the Word of God? Why or why not?

BRANDS FROM THE BURNING

1. Pick out some of the details in Jeremiah's description of God's judgment of Israel that show how terrible the situation was.

2. How does this judgment show God's attitude toward sin and spiritual idolatry?

3. What will happen in God's final judgment on the earth?

4. Will God "leave behind, ignore, forget, misplace, or lose a single believer" in the final judgment to come? Explain.

5. In view of this coming terrible judgment, what is your responsibility?

NOTES

INTRODUCTION: JEREMIAH'S TIMES AND OUR TIMES

1. Francis A. Schaeffer, *Death in the City* (Downers Grove, Ill.: InterVarsity, 1969), 70.
2. C. S. Lewis, "De Descriptione Temporum," in *Selected Literary Essays,* Walter Hooper, ed. (Cambridge: Cambridge University Press, 1967), 1-14 (5).

CHAPTER 1: GOD FILES FOR DIVORCE

1. Sheldon Vanauken, *A Severe Mercy* (London: Hodder and Stoughton, 1977; repr. 1989), 29.
2. R. K. Harrison, *Jeremiah and Lamentations,* Tyndale Old Testament Commentaries (Downers Grove, Ill.: InterVarsity, 1973), 60.
3. K. E. Bailey and W. L. Holladay, "The 'Young Camel' and 'Wild Ass' in Jer. 2:23-25," *Vetus Testamentum* 18 (1968), 258-9.
4. Bailey and Holladay, "The 'Young Camel,'" 259.
5. Raymond Ortlund, Jr., *A Passion for God* (Wheaton, Ill.: Crossway, 1994), 205.
6. Ibid., 205-6.

CHAPTER 2: A GOOD MAN IS HARD TO FIND

1. R. K. Harrison, *Jeremiah and Lamentations,* Tyndale Old Testament Commentaries (Downers Grove, Ill.: InterVarsity, 1973), 74.
2. Os Guinness and John Seel, eds., *No God But God: Breaking with the Idols of Our Age* (Chicago: Moody, 1992).
3. A. J. David Richards, Professor of Law, New York University.
4. *Time,* May 27, 1996, 17.
5. William Foxwell Albright, *The Archaeology of Palestine* (New York: Penguin, 1949), 141-2.

CHAPTER 3: AT THE CROSSROADS

1. Cited in James Montgomery Boice, *Two Cities, Two Loves: Christian Responsibility in a Crumbling Culture* (Downers Grove, Ill.: InterVarsity, 1996), 74.
2. Oscar Handlin, "The Unmarked Way," *The American Scholar* (Summer 1996), 335-55 (335).
3. Quoted by A. A. Hodge in *The Life of Charles Hodge* (New York, 1880), 521.
4. Johanna McGeary, "The Right Way to Peace?" *Time,* June 10, 1996, 30-36 (30).
5. See, for example, William L. Holladay, *Jeremiah 1: A Commentary on the Book of the*

Prophet Jeremiah, Chapters 1-25, Hermeneia (Philadelphia: Fortress, 1986), 223; or Douglas Rawlinson Jones, *Jeremiah,* New Century Bible Commentary (Grand Rapids, Mich.: Eerdmans, 1992), 137.

6. John Guest, *Jeremiah, Lamentations,* The Communicator's Commentary (Waco, Tex.: Word, 1988), 69.

CHAPTER 4: WHAT THE CHURCH NEEDS NOW IS REFORMATION

1. Pope Leo X, *Exsurge Domine* (1520), in Roland H. Bainton, *Here I Stand: A Life of Martin Luther* (New York: Abingdon, 1950), 147.

2. John Calvin, *A Commentary on Jeremiah,* 5 vols. (Edinburgh: Banner of Truth, 1989), 4:366.

3. Robert Davidson, *Jeremiah,* Daily Study Bible, 2 vols. (Philadelphia: Westminster, 1983), 1:73.

CHAPTER 5: SOMETHING TO BOAST ABOUT

1. John Calvin, *A Commentary on Jeremiah,* 5 vols. (Edinburgh: Banner of Truth, 1989), 1:496.

2. Henry Wadsworth Longfellow, "The Reaper and the Flowers," in Robert Davidson, *Jeremiah,* Daily Study Bible, 2 vols. (Philadelphia: Westminster, 1983), 1:90.

3. Page H. Kelley, *Jeremiah 1-25,* Word Biblical Commentary (Dallas: Word, 1991), 148.

4. J. A. Thompson, *The Book of Jeremiah,* New International Commentary on the Old Testament (Grand Rapids, Mich.: Eerdmans, 1980), 316.

5. Francis A. Schaeffer, *Death in the City* (Downers Grove, Ill.: InterVarsity, 1969), 71.

6. Thomas Jefferson Hogg, *The Life of Percy Bysshe Shelley* (London, 1858).

7. Calvin, *Jeremiah,* 1:503.

CHAPTER 6: THE SCARECROW IN THE MELON PATCH

1. Derek Kidner, *The Message of Jeremiah: Against Wind and Tide,* The Bible Speaks Today (Downers Grove, Ill.: InterVarsity, 1987), 56.

2. John Calvin, *Institutes of the Christian Religion,* John T. McNeill, ed., Ford Lewis Battles, trans., 2 vols., Library of Christian Classics, 20-21 (Philadelphia: Westminster, 1960), I.11.3.

3. David F. Wells, *God in the Wasteland* (Grand Rapids, Mich.: Eerdmans, 1994), 52.

4. Calvin, *Institutes,* I.11.8.

5. Richard Keyes, "The Idol Factory," in Os Guinness and John Seel, eds., *No God But God: Breaking with the Idols of Our Age* (Chicago: Moody, 1992), 29-48 (38).

6. Keyes, "The Idol Factory," 33.

CHAPTER 7: IN THE POTTER'S HANDS

1. William Shakespeare, *The Tragedy of Hamlet, Prince of Denmark,* William W. Main, ed. (New York: Odyssey, 1963), V.1.

2. John Calvin, *A Commentary on Jeremiah,* 5 vols. (Edinburgh: Banner of Truth, 1989), 2:393.

3. J. A. Thompson, *The Book of Jeremiah,* New International Commentary on the Old Testament (Grand Rapids, Mich.: Eerdmans, 1980), 433.

4. Eugene H. Peterson, *Run with the Horses: The Quest for Life at Its Best* (Downers Grove, Ill.: InterVarsity, 1983), 77.

5. F. B. Meyer, *Jeremiah: Priest and Prophet,* rev. edn. (Fort Washington, Penn.: Christian Literature Crusade, 1993), 80.

6. Samuel Macauley Jackson, *Huldreich Zwingli, the Reformer of German Switzerland* (New York: G. P. Putnam's Sons, 1901), 148.

CHAPTER 8: DARK NIGHT OF THE SOUL

1. Kathleen Norris, *The Cloister Walk* (New York: Riverhead, 1996), 31.
2. Ibid., 31-35.
3. John Calvin, *A Commentary on Jeremiah*, 5 vols. (Edinburgh: Banner of Truth, 1989), 3:38.
4. Dietrich Bonhoeffer, quoted in Robert Davidson, *Jeremiah*, Daily Study Bible, 2 vols. (Philadelphia: Westminster, 1983), 1:165.
5. Compare Jeremiah 20:16 with Genesis 19:24-28.
6. R. E. O. White, *The Indomitable Prophet* (Grand Rapids, Mich.: Eerdmans, 1992), 162.
7. Calvin, *Commentary on Jeremiah*, 3:44.
8. Derek Kidner, *The Message of Jeremiah: Against Wind and Tide*, The Bible Speaks Today (Downers Grove, Ill.: InterVarsity, 1987), 81.
9. J. G. McConville, *Judgment and Promise: An Interpretation of the Book of Jeremiah* (Leicester, England: Apollos, 1993), 73-4.

CHAPTER 9: THE BEST-MADE PLANS

1. Robert C. Linthicum, *City of God, City of Satan: A Biblical Theology of the Urban Church* (Grand Rapids, Mich.: Zondervan, 1991), 145.
2. Quoted in Harvie M. Conn, *The American City and the Evangelical Church* (Grand Rapids, Mich.: Baker, 1994), 31.
3. Quoted in Conn, *American City*, 38.
4. Augustine, *The City of God*, Philip Schaff, ed., *Nicene and Post-Nicene Fathers*, First Series, vol. 2 (Peabody, Mass.: Hendrickson, 1994), XV.1.
5. James M. Boice, *Two Cities, Two Loves: Christian Responsibility in a Crumbling Culture* (Downers Grove, Ill.: InterVarsity, 1996), 35.
6. Pieter Bos, "City Cries," in Floyd McClung, *Seeing the City with the Eyes of God* (Tarrytown, N.Y.: Revell, 1991), 72.
7. Roger S. Greenway and Timothy M. Monsma, *Cities: Mission's New Frontier* (Grand Rapids, Mich.: Baker, 1989), 44.
8. Ronald J. Sider, "The State of Evangelical Social Concern, 1978," *Evangelical Newsletter*, Vol. 5, No. 13 (June 30, 1978).
9. John Perkins, *With Justice for All* (Ventura, Calif.: Regal, 1982), 65.
10. John Bright, *Jeremiah*, Anchor Bible (Garden City, N.Y.: Doubleday, 1965), 206.
11. Jacques Ellul, *The Meaning of the City* (Grand Rapids, Mich.: Eerdmans, 1970), 181.
12. See Paul Volz, *Der Prophet Jeremia, Kommentar Zum Alten Testament*, 10 (Leipzig: Deichert, 1928), 269.
13. See Linthicum, *City of God*, 149-53.

CHAPTER 10: THE NEW COVENANT

1. O. Palmer Robertson, *The Christ of the Covenants* (Phillipsburg, N.J.: Presbyterian and Reformed, 1980), 4.
2. John Murray, *The Covenant of Grace* (Phillipsburg, N.J.: Presbyterian and Reformed, 1953), 31.
3. Robert Davidson, *Jeremiah and Lamentations*, 2 vols., Daily Study Bible (Philadelphia: Westminster, 1985), 2:88.
4. Herman Witsius, *The Economy of the Covenants between God and Man*, 2 vols. (London, 1773; repr. Escondido, Calif.: Den Dulk Christian Foundation, 1990), I.1.9.
5. Gerhard Von Rad, *Old Testament Theology*, D. M. G. Stalker, trans., 2 vols. (New York: Harper & Row, 1960), 2:213.

6. J. A. Thompson, *The Book of Jeremiah*, New International Commentary on the Old Testament (Grand Rapids, Mich.: Eerdmans, 1980), 580.

7. Robertson, *Christ of the Covenants*, 281.

8. F. B. Huey, Jr., *Jeremiah, Lamentations*, The New American Commentary (Nashville, Tenn.: Broadman, 1993), 279.

9. R. K. Harrison, *Jeremiah and Lamentations*, Tyndale Old Testament Commentaries (Downers Grove, Ill.: InterVarsity, 1973), 140.

10. John Calvin, *A Commentary on Jeremiah*, 5 vols. (Edinburgh: Banner of Truth, 1989), 4:130.

11. Ibid., 4:126.

12. Robertson, *Christ of the Covenants*, 190.

13. Quoted in *Urban Mission* (June 1997), 30.

14. Jonathan Edwards, *The Works of Jonathan Edwards*, 2 vols. (Edinburgh: Banner of Truth, 1974), 2:765.

15. Murray, *Covenant of Grace*, 31.

16. Thompson, *Book of Jeremiah*, 581.

17. Oliver O'Donovan, *The Desire of the Nations: Rediscovering the Roots of Political Theology* (Cambridge University Press, 1996), 285.

18. Thomas Boston, *The Complete Works of the Late Rev. Thomas Boston*, Ettrick, Samuel M'Millan, ed., 12 vols. (London, 1853; repr. Wheaton, Ill.: Richard Owen Roberts, 1980), 8:430.

CHAPTER 11: BUYER'S MARKET

1. William L. Ventolo, Jr., and Martha R. Williams, *Fundamentals of Real Estate Appraisal*, 6th edn. (Chicago: Dearborn Financial Publishing, 1994), 59.

2. Walter Brueggemann, *To Build, To Plant: A Commentary on Jeremiah 26-52*, International Theological Commentary (Grand Rapids, Mich.: Eerdmans, 1991), 79.

3. John Calvin, *A Commentary on Jeremiah*, 5 vols. (Edinburgh: Banner of Truth, 1989), 4:160.

4. Titus Livius Pataviensis, *From the Founding of the City*, Aubrey de Sélincourt, trans. (Baltimore, Md.: Penguin, 1965), XXVI.11 (368).

5. Derek Kidner, *The Message of Jeremiah: Against Wind and Tide*, The Bible Speaks Today (Downers Grove, Ill.: InterVarsity, 1987), 112.

6. Calvin, *Jeremiah*, 4:168.

7. Kidner, *Message of Jeremiah*, 113.

8. Quoted in Phillip E. Johnson, *Reason in the Balance: The Case Against Naturalism in Science, Law and Education* (Downers Grove, Ill.: InterVarsity, 1995), 12-13.

9. Ibid., 7-8.

10. John Calvin, *Institutes of the Christian Religion*, John T. McNeill, ed., Ford Lewis Battles, trans., 2 vols., Library of Christian Classics, 20-21 (Philadelphia: Westminster, 1960).

11. John Guest, *Jeremiah, Lamentations*, The Communicator's Commentary (Waco, Tex.: Word, 1988), 234.

CHAPTER 12: BOOK BURNING

1. Thomas Watson, *A Body of Divinity*, rev. edn. (London, 1692; repr. Edinburgh: Banner of Truth, 1965), 27.

2. John Guest, *Jeremiah, Lamentations*, The Communicator's Commentary (Waco, Tex.: Word, 1988), 253.

3. Derek Kidner, *The Message of Jeremiah: Against Wind and Tide*, The Bible Speaks Today (Downers Grove, Ill.: InterVarsity, 1987), 119.

4. *God's Word Today,* P.O. Box 2000, Philadelphia, Penn. 19103.

5. Small Groups Ministries International, 8776 Driftwood Drive, Riverside, Calif. 92503.

6. Gemariah is one of the biblical figures whose existence can be confirmed from extra-biblical sources. A clay document marker (bulla) found near Jerusalem in 1983 reads: "belonging to Gemariah, son of Shaphan the scribe." See Y. Shiloh, "A Group of Hebrew Bullae from the City of David," *Israel Exploration Journal* 36 (1986), 16-38.

7. J. I. Packer, sermon on Jeremiah 36 preached c. 1990 at Westminster Theological Seminary, Philadelphia.

8. J. I. Packer, *Truth and Power: The Place of Scripture in the Christian Life* (Wheaton, Ill.: Harold Shaw, 1996).

9. *Westminster Confession of Faith* (Philadelphia: Great Commission Publications, n.d.), I.8.

10. *Hall's Chronicle: Containing the History of England* (London, 1809), 762-3, quoted in David Daniell, *William Tyndale: A Biography* (New Haven, Conn.: Yale University Press, 1994), 196-7.

CHAPTER 13: BRANDS FROM THE BURNING

1. John Guest, *Jeremiah, Lamentations,* The Communicator's Commentary (Waco, Tex: Word, 1988), 277. See also Flavius Josephus, "The Antiquities of the Jews," in *The Works of Josephus,* William Whiston, trans. (Peabody, Mass.: Hendrickson, 1987), X.8.1-5.

2. See J. A. Thompson, *The Book of Jeremiah,* New International Commentary on the Old Testament (Grand Rapids, Mich.: Eerdmans, 1980), 647.

3. John Calvin, *A Commentary on Jeremiah,* 5 vols. (Edinburgh: Banner of Truth, 1989), 4:421.

4. John Blanchard, *Whatever Happened to Hell?* (Durham, U.K.: Evangelical Press, 1993). See also the chapter "On Banishing the Lake of Fire" in D. A. Carson, *The Gagging of God: Christianity Confronts Pluralism* (Grand Rapids, Mich.: Zondervan, 1996), 515-36.

5. Walter Brueggemann, *To Build, to Plant: A Commentary on Jeremiah 26-52,* International Theological Commentary (Grand Rapids, Mich.: Eerdmans, 1991), 156.

6. William Shakespeare, *The Tragedy of King Lear,* Tucker Brooke and William Lyon Phelps, eds. (New Haven, Conn.: Yale University Press, 1947), III.7.

7. F. B. Huey, Jr., *Jeremiah, Lamentations,* The New American Commentary (Nashville, Tenn.: Broadman, 1993), 346.

8. Charles Wesley, "The Wesleys' Conversion Hymn," in J. I. Packer, *Knowing God* (Downers Grove, Ill.: InterVarsity, 1973), 189.

9. Thomas Boston, *Human Nature in its Fourfold State* (Edinburgh: Banner of Truth, 1964), 505-6.

GENERAL INDEX

SCRIPTURE INDEX